BANKING PROBLEMS AND THEIR SOLUTIONS

A note to readers

The material which appears in this book, covering the years 1961-70, first appeared in *The Bankers' Magazine*. A similar volume, covering the years 1971-80, is in the course of preparation and should be available in 1981.

Banking problems and their solutions

Compiled and edited by

F. R. Ryder, LL.B., F.I.B.

of Gray's Inn, Barrister at Law, Gilbart lecturer,
1970-1971.

WATERLOW (LONDON) LIMITED 1980

Banking Problems and their Solutions
Second (Revised) Edition 1980

©Printed and published in Great Britain by
Waterlow (London) Limited,
Holywell House, Worship Street,
London EC2A 2EN
ISBN 0 900 791 61 6

Contents

Prefaces – pages 8 & 9

PART ONE : THE PAYING BANKER – page 11

Introduction
1 : Priority in paying standing orders
2 : A cheque drawn with notation *subject to contract*
3 : The paying banker and mental incapacity
4 : Choice of which cheque to pay
5 : Encashing a crossed cheque
6 : Cheques drawn on a former bank
7 : A benevolent society mandate
8 : A garnishee order and uncleared effects
9 : Appointment of a receiver and late returns

PART TWO : THE COLLECTING BANKER – page 37

Introduction
1 : Delay in collecting a cheque
2 : Fraudulent reference as to customer's identity
3 : Collecting a cheque payable to a solicitor's client
4 : Collecting a third party cheque
5 : The customer's responsibility for cheques collected for his account
6 : Conversion of a cheque obtained by a customer by fraud
7 : Presumption of payment of cheque tendered for collection
8 : Cheque crossed *Account payee only*

PART THREE : BILLS AND NEGOTIATION OF CHEQUES – Page 62

Introduction
1 : Attempted re-acceptance of a bill
2 : Liability on a transferred cheque
3 : The banker as a holder for value
4 : The rights of the holder of a stopped cheque

PART FOUR : GUARANTEES – page 74

Introduction
1 : Guarantors and a preferential debt
2 : Set-off against guarantor
3 : The duration of a guarantee
4 : A bankrupt guarantor

PART FIVE : BANKER AND CUSTOMER – page 87

Introduction
1 : An overdraft repayable on demand
2 : Husband's and wife's securities in one deed box
3 : An incorrect bank statement
4 : Chattels of the fugitive customer
5 : Enquiry as to fate of cheque tendered for a third party credit
6 : Agreeing not to answer status enquiries
7 : Commitments and outstanding cheques after demand for repayment
8 : A banker's enquiry and mistaken identity
9 : Full information on a banker's enquiry
10 : Combining accounts
11 : Clearing rules and the customer
12 : A customer's mental incapacity

PART SIX : MORTGAGES – page 124

Introduction
1 : A land certificate obtained by fraud
2 : A share in a house as security
3 : Proceeds of a fire claim as security
4 : The wife's title to mortgaged property
5 : Notice of second mortgage
6 : Undertaking from a housing association
7 : Forged deeds

PART SEVEN : MISCELLANEOUS SECURITIES – page 145

Introduction
1 : Implications of a loan postponement
2 : Children and National Savings Certificates
3 : A banker's lien and a joint and several liability
4 : The proceeds of a fire policy
5 : A matured life policy

PART EIGHT : COMPANIES – page 159

Introduction
1 : Fraud by a signatory on a company's account
2 : One banking account for a group of companies
3 : Bank holding floating charge ousting judgment creditor
4 : Solicitors' undertaking on behalf of a company
5 : Rival claims of a company and its director to mortgaged property
6 : A petition because of directors' quarrels
7 : A wages preferential claim

PART NINE : MISCELLANEOUS PROBLEMS – page 181

Introduction
1 : Credit transfer and a dishonoured cheque
2 : Dishonour of a banker's payment
3 : Revoking a credit transfer
4 : Credit transfer on the strength of a cheque
5 : The customer awaiting trial
6 : A safe custody problem

7

Preface

For a number of years past we have had frequent requests for the publication of a collected edition of the monthly banking problems with the winning answers, which have been a feature of *The Bankers' Magazine* since 1927. It has been recognised, however, that to be useful to bankers the volume had to be something more than a mere reprint. Inevitably changes in the law and the practice of banking – the latter greater in the past decade than in any in living memory – had to be reflected. Consequently the answers extending for some ten years past have been edited and entirely re-set in order to produce a currently accurate collection. As readers of *The Bankers' Magazine* well know, the topics arising in the problems are very varied. Some are of obviously wide importance, others savour of the curious. Most have undoubtedly occurred in practice; even those few that may have the fruits of fertile imagination probably reflect discussions among bankers – or between students and teachers – stemming from actual events of a germane character.

It was also felt that, as with any collection, there was an absence of background. The troublesome, disturbing, odd, and interesting problems of daily banking life cannot be expected to provide in themselves a complete guide to the subject. In order, however, that without reference to text books the problems should be seen in the light of standard law and practice each of the groups into which the answers have been divided has been preceded by a note summarising very briefly indeed the established law and practice. Thus the book provides two extremes : on the one hand a simple statement much shorter than a study note on each topic concerned; on the other hand discussion and answers relating to practical problems sufficiently unusual – and perhaps complex – to have caused them to be sent to *The Bankers' Magazine*. Most of the questions relate to problems that could well be litigated if enough were at stake; it must therefore be appreciated that the 'solutions' often represent what is thought to be 'the better view'. If the answers had absolutely incontrovertible solutions they would have little interest as problems.

F.R.R.

1971

Preface to Second Edition

The complete sell-out of the First Edition reflects the practical bent of bankers who are more interested in the resolution of problems than of the legal principles underlying the situations. Yet of course, any compromise is inevitably associated with what would happen if the matter went to court – and with the costs likely to be involved.

The few amendments made stem for the most part from the attempts being made by Parliament and the courts to protect the uninitiated from the professional – a trend that may go too far if that has not happened already.

F.R.R.

September, 1980.

Part one : The paying banker

The position of the paying banker is in some senses an accident of history. Long before cheques were known the bill of exchange was in existence. When, through the goldsmiths the relation between banker and customer gradually developed, the document by which the customer withdrew money from his banker, or instructed his banker to pay money away to a third party, became of the type coming within the category of a bill of exchange. Thus, to appreciate the subject clearly, there is a dual aspect to be noted :

(a) first, the rights and duties of the paying banker are to be ascertained by reference to the banker-customer contract, and,

(b) secondly, the rights of the parties and of third parties are affected because the document used is a form of bill of exchange, a cheque being a bill of exchange drawn on a banker payable on demand.

The circumstances in which the banker has a duty to his customer and in which the customer in turn has obligations to his banker are examined in detail in Part 5 dealing with the banker/customer relationship. The consequences of the instrument by which money is withdrawn from a banking account being a bill of exchange are to be seen in the rights of a collecting banker who becomes holder in due course of a cheque, see Part 3, *Bills and negotiation of cheques*. In addition, the parties involved in relation to a cheque, the holder, the drawer, the drawee, and the payee are affected by the provisions of the Bills of Exchange Act. Some of these sections are for the protection of the banker. The paying banker is protected by Section 60 of the Bills of Exchange Act relating to the payment of cheques and again by Section 80 in relation to the payment of crossed cheques, and even further by Section 1 of the Cheques Act 1957. This latter Statute specifically covers instruments used to withdraw money or instruct a banker to pay away money which fail to conform to the requirement of the definition of a bill of exchange. These may be conditional orders and, therefore, strictly in law equitable assignments and not bills of exchange. In Scotland a cheque is regarded as an assignment of funds and the party having notice of such assignment may not pay away any funds in his hands. Thus a banker having a balance that is insufficient to pay

11

a cheque in Scotland must hold the balance for the benefit of a third party in whose favour a cheque has been drawn and presented. It now *appears* that it is no longer always enough for the paying banker to obey implicitly a company customer's mandate; if it is evident to the banker's knowledge that the payment is illegal he will have a responsibility to the company itself (to a liquidator, for instance, for any loss sustained).

From the specific questions the following points are of interest:

Question 1
The whole question of the priority of the payment of standing orders is quite confused. The one determining factor that is certain beyond doubt is that if a course of business is established with a particular customer a banker will need to obtain very clear evidence before he departs from the course of business. More and more are customers being persuaded, or coerced to agree to 'Direct Debiting'.

Question 2
'Subject to contract' is a phrase much more frequently used in relation to the payment of deposits than on a cheque. Nevertheless the point was raised and is likely to have been incorporated as a reservation.

Question 3
Mental incapacity in practice is often a difficult problem. It is, however, very seldom that a banker or third party will be assailed by a Receiver because of anything that he has done in good faith, notwithstanding some knowledge of the mental incapacity. However, the practical guidance indicated in the answer is helpful.

Question 4
The choice of which cheque to pay has been a regular question of enquiry among bankers for many years. No-one has yet indicated any ground that would prevent the banker paying which he wishes. Sometimes, of course, a business interest may affect a decision. The customer, however, is basically embarrassed because he is at fault in drawing cheques that go beyond the amount standing to his credit.

Question 5
The encashment of a crossed cheque is a commonplace example of where a banker acts on the strength of his customer's specific instruction to disregard a crossing. Of course, where that specific authority proves to be a false authority the banker is appropriately embarrassed.

Question 6
This is a very practical question showing the need for care when an account is transferred from one bank to another.

Question 7
This question is essentially technical and it cannot be emphasised too strongly that the answer may depend on the rules of the particular Society.

Question 8
Garnishee problems are among the most difficult. This is no exception and it must be admitted that the answer is controversial.

Question 9
The answer here is somewhat rambling, but is closely associated with the Clearing House Rules and payment and collection of cheques, which is the quintessence of modern banking. There is an Australian case *Riedell v Commercial Bank of Australia* (1931, VLR 382) in which a bank was held responsible to its customer when it accepted gratuitously a 'late return' of a cheque that it was collecting for that customer.

1 : Priority in paying standing orders

Your customer has a small current account and has given you a standing order for £7 payable on 5th monthly in favour of a hire purchase company. On 5 January the balance on the account is £1 only and consequently the standing order is not paid. A cash credit of £10 is paid in on 20 January, without comment. In the absence of any special arrangement with your customer, should the bank now pay the £7 due on 5 January or hold the order until 5 February? If the bank pays the order on 20 January and a cheque for £10 is presented on 25th which is returned unpaid through lack of funds, what are the legal implications? Is the position altered by the fact that if the January instalment had been paid, your customer would have paid the hire purchase company one-third of the hire purchase price?

Three problems are involved in the question, the first two being interrelated. It is however desirable first to consider the nature of a standing order. It states that items are to be paid successively and, even if the rest of the document conforms with the requirements of a bill of exchange, it could not be considered as being within this classification because there is no fixed total amount. A bill can indicate that payment is to be by stated instalments but a standing order contains no total sum. The next question is to ascertain its character legally. All orders to pay money that are not bills of exchange, such as conditional orders, are in law, it would seem certain, assignments – more precisely informal or equitable assignments on which the recipient has no right to sue in his own name but which give him a claim on the money, if the banker has notice. There is a possibility that, strictly speaking, a banker in England has to treat such an order in the same way as a banker in Scotland treats a cheque. If he has a lesser sum available this has to be reserved for the beneficiary of the equitable assignment of which the banker has undoubtedly notice by reason of its presentation (or in the case of a standing order, by reason of its possession). This principle is thought to apply however only to the extent that monies are in possession of the banker at the time he gets notice which is when the order is presented or comes up for payment. The mere possession of such a document (as with a standing order) might be regarded as earlier notice but this thought gives

14

rise to much legal difficulty and is not directly relevant to the problem. For it has to be remembered that the document is, in the same way as a cheque, a feature of the banker-customer contract, in that it is a service offered – on which offers are invited and accepted. To that extent the obligations are consensual and not alone that of the banker·

It has to be presumed when answering the question that there has been, of course, no special arrangement between banker and customer about what to do in such circumstances and, also, of more practical possibility, that there has not been a course of dealing well established that a standing order should or should not be paid when the balance is insufficient. In the absence of such express or implied agreement the position is dominated by the fact that the customer is in breach of contract, although a cheque overdrawing an account without arrangement may be regarded by the banker as an offer to borrow; to give an instruction when insufficient funds are available is probably technically a breach of contract. As Lord Atkin said in the case of *Joachimson* v. *Swiss Banking Corporation* (1921) 3 K.B. 110 a term of the contract is the payment of cheques within the credit balance. Cheques drawn in excess can certainly be ignored in the absence of an express or implied agreement for an overdraft and there is much to be said for the view that to draw a cheque for which there is no provision is a breach of contract. (*Sometimes* here, as is well known, and *always* in some countries, it is criminal.) Similarly the giving of a standing order and the failure to provide funds would probably be a breach on the part of the customer. When a customer has drawn a cheque without funds or failed to provide sufficient balance to pay the standing order it is difficult to see how he can claim successfully that the banker is in breach, whether in the case in question the banker elects to pay the standing order and dishonour the cheque or to pay the cheque, having ignored the standing order. The customer is at a disadvantage in that it is his action that will have brought about the situation; and it is consistent with the view that the banker is immune from a claim whichever he does–that one has not heard of an action arising out of such a situation, which is not infrequent in practice.

The significance of the failure to pay an amount that would have caused a total of two-thirds to have been paid on hire purchase standing order is that, if the bank was liable, the damage could be increased because prior to that time the ability to seize and sell is free from the statutory rights becoming available to the hirer when this one-third has been paid. This would have to be however a seizure and not merely the vulnerability to a seizure·

2 : A cheque drawn with notation
subject to contract

Midtown Bank Ltd. receives a cheque in the clearing for £25 (technically correct) and boldly printed by the customer's own hand under the words of the amount is subject to contract. *This appears on the face of the cheque, and there are no markings on the reverse. Do these words constitute a condition, and if so, what matters should the paying bankers (Midtown Bank) take into consideration before cancelling the cheque, or might they even send it back?*

It is of course unusual to find the expression *subject to contract* on a cheque, although it is commonplace in correspondence prior to the creation of a contract, particularly in relation to the sale of houses. Most people who have had the occasion to buy or sell property are aware that despite the payment of a deposit the other party is not bound if the deposit has been paid *subject to contract,* which words are likely to be found on the receipt as well as in any relevant correspondence. In fact if X agrees to sell and Y agrees to buy without such reservation (or some similar proviso such as *subject to survey*) there is a binding contract, known as an 'open contract'. This must be written and signed by the party sought to be bound and contain the essential details of price, parties and identification. There is a further reason that such arrangements are nearly always conditioned by reservation and not binding until a more formal document is prepared. This is because where there is an open contract there is a strict obligation on the vendor to make title. Frequently owners are not able to do this in that there are either covenants relating to user of the premises or minor insignificant infelicities in title which have to be mentioned specifically in the contract. The leading case is *Winn* v. *Bull* (1877) 7 Ch.D.29.

The problem itself involves the relationship between the customer and the banker and the customer and the payee.

Regarding the relationship of banker and customer the points to be considered are whether the proviso makes the document conditional and, secondly, whether the banker is concerned at all. There are a number of cases from which it is clear that the courts are willing to regard as incidental notations on cheques that would otherwise make the document conditional. For example in *Nathan* v. *Ogden's Ltd.* (1905) 93 L.T. 126 a note at the bottom of the cheque that the receipt on the back must be signed was regarded as being only a note to the payee. Similarly in *Roberts* v. *Marsh* (1915) 1 K.B. 42 an annotation that the cheque 'was to be retained' it being intended to substitute a new cheque was considered as not making the cheque conditional. Again a cheque drawn 'in full settlement' possibly does not concern the banker now that endorsements are not required. Thus in the absence of any contrary arrangement – express, or implied by a course of dealing – it is virtually certain that the words *subject to contract* may be ignored. It is known, of course, as mentioned, as a common condition imposed to characterise non-binding communications between a respective vendor and purchaser.

So far as relates to the relationship between the drawer and the recipient the words are a *prima facie* indication that the payment is conditional, as with a deposit on a house. In fact so long as the cheque, or even its photograph, is available it would be sufficient evidence to enable the drawer to recover the money paid from the payee, provided the cheque could be proved to have reached him. It is interesting to notice that in the recent case of *Burnett* v. *Westminster Bank* (1965) 3 AER 81 Mocatta, J., indicated that he would consider a reference on a cheque itself as being sufficient notice from a banker to a customer.

B

3 : The paying banker and mental incapacity

Mr Smith has had a well-conducted account ta the X Bank for
many years with an average credit balance of £250. Recently
stocks were sold and the balance is now £4,000. Mrs Smith now
approaches the bank manager and says that Mr Smith has been
a voluntary patient at a mental institution which he left of his
own accord and that he has expressed his intention of giving away
his money. She anticipates that he will draw cheques for this
purpose which she asks the bank not to pay because her husband's
mind is unbalanced. What should the bank manager do if on
the following day two cheques are presented, one for £500 in favour
of a local charity and the other for £1,000 in favour of J. Robinson,
who is unknown to the bank manager?

Most important to the banker is the evidence he receives of his customer's alleged incapacity. As a general rule of contract, a person
dealing with someone who is insane is not deprived of his rights against
that party unless it can be shown that the former was aware of the
mental incapacity of the latter. Mere hearsay evidence, or even the
view of a member of the customer's family, is of course insufficient.
Although some forms of mental illness are reflected by an abnormal
generosity or extreme parsimony these signs do not provide any reliable
evidence. They may make the banker's task more difficult.

The question is whether the customer is regarded as able to understand the nature of a business transaction. Fortunately this decision
is one that the banker does not have to make. The banker should
seek a doctor's view. If it can be obtained in writing it is desirable
but, if not, a note should be made of any oral intimation in the branch
record book or diary *at the time* the information is received. If the
doctor is *unable* to say that the customer *cannot* understand the nature
of a business transaction, then it is inconceivable that the banker could
be assailed successfully for paying cheques. The decision is one for the
doctor but mental incapacity should not be associated with physical
violence. People unlikely to do physical harm to themselves or to anyone
else may be unable to understand a business transaction through men-

18

tal incapacity. Similarly it is just possible that persons forcibly incarcerated and physically violent may be able to understand business matters, but where a person is certified for the purpose of physical restraint one obviously would be justified in requiring *positive* evidence before paying cheques. Normally in such a case a receiver will be appointed who is legally the only person who can handle the customer's affairs.

On applying the above principles to the facts of the question, it is clear that the banker cannot rely on the wife's views and statements. He should however seek views of the customer's doctor or the medical superintendent of the home where the customer has been a patient. Possibly the wife will be able to assist in arranging for such an opinion. If the cheques are received before this can be obtained, the banker cannot be sued for paying the cheques. If he returns the cheques, in case it eventuates to have been unjustified, then he should mark them 'Refer to Drawer'. Although this answer legally is safe, there is, of course, the popular conception that it means an absence of funds. One could perhaps therefore use a different answer such as 'Drawer's Mandate requires verification'. This would be ambiguous, but possibly preferred by the relatives and the customer. An incorrect reference to mental incapacity is libellous and could increase the damages.

One further thought is that if the cheque in favour of the charity is paid and the bank successfully attacked, the payment, being voluntary, is likely to be recoverable legally (*Re Diplock*, 1948, 2 All E.R. 318).

4 : Choice of which cheque to pay

A, who was formerly on the staff of a bank, is now a farmer and B,
his brother is a car dealer who runs his own hire purchase. Both
have dealings with C, another farmer who is paying B by banker's
order £25 on 15th of each month.
   On 15 January C's cheque to A for £24 is returned 'refer to drawer'
A is aware of C's commitment to B and is angered on learning
that on 16 January the monthly payment was made to B (the
account of C having that day been provided with sufficient
cash funds). Has either A or C any right of action against the bank?
Would C have had any such right if the cheque had been
re-presented on 16 January and again returned?

The first point is that, normally, a banker is not liable to anyone other
than his customer. He can choose to pay which of two cheques he
likes and even his customer cannot criticise him because his customer
is in breach of his contract by drawing a cheque that would overdraw
the account without any previous arrangement. There are exceptions.
If there had been a special arrangement with the bank or a credit has
been earmarked, the banker is obliged to honour his arrangement.
There is one other possible exception. The form of cheque may amount
to a conditional order that is probably notice of an assignment. A
cheque is treated in such a way in Scotland, and attaches a balance
insufficient to meet it.
   Turning to the case in question, and taking first the position of C,
in the absence of any special arrangement with the bank he cannot
complain. He has drawn a cheque and given an instruction, *both* of
which cannot be honoured, and he is at fault. It may be that if
similar circumstances have arisen in the past and the bank has always
paid the cheque, the customer perhaps has some right. He is, however,
in breach of contract and should not have drawn the cheque; therefore
it is very improbable that he can benefit from any previous course of
dealings. A has no contractual relationship with the bank and has no
rights. If the 'cheque' were conditional in form, it is possible that as
an equitable assignee he would be able to claim such credit balance

(obviously less than £24) as existed on 15 January. He would not, however, have any rights beyond that. It is possible, although unusual, for a cheque to be conditional and therefore an assignment. Then it is only the balance, if any, at the time of first presentation that A could claim.

It is difficult to see that the time of re-presentation of the cheque could affect the position of the parties. If A has any right to the small balance, which is extremely unlikely, that right arises at first presentation; C's position is unaffected by the re-presentation.

5 : Encashing a crossed cheque

A customer of Hightown branch gives the following instruction:
'Please instruct your Lowtown branch to cash my cheques in
favour of myself to the extent of £100 in any one month.'
This instruction is passed on to the Lowtown branch. The customer
draws and endorses a crossed *cheque, intending to cash it. The*
cheque is stolen. Lowtown branch cash it for the thief.
What is the bank's position? Would it have been different if the
cheque, uncrossed, *had been paid to a shopkeeper who*
had innocently cashed it for the thief?

The position of a banker paying a cheque under a 'credit opened' or
more precisely a clean credit, where the drawer is a customer of another branch, is the subject of an answer in *Questions on Banking
Practice* No 399 (9th Edition). (This does not appear in the Xth
Edition.) The specific point has not been before the Courts but the
answer to the above mentioned question incorporates a Counsel's
Opinion taken by the Institute of Bankers in 1923. This makes it
clear that such payment at another branch, *where there has been
an arrangement,* may be in the ordinary course of business.
Similarly, it is obvious that the mere fact that a cheque is drawn
on the branch by whom the special arrangement is made cannot
be regarded as involving negligence. Section 60 of the Bills of Exchange Act relieves a banker paying a cheque bearing a forged or
unauthorised endorsement from the onus of showing that such an
endorsement is genuine and fully authorised if payment is in good faith
and in the ordinary course of business. Section 80 of the same Act protects a banker paying such a cheque if he acts in good faith and without negligence only provided that he pays in accordance with the crossing. Section 1 of the Cheques Act, 1957, if it applies, requires that
payment shall be in the ordinary course of business.

Thus, turning to the question specifically, payment is not in accordance with the crossing because payment has not been made to another banker. Similarly, it is *not* in the ordinary course of business
to pay a crossed cheque to someone other than another banker. There-

fore the banker cannot debit the customer's account with the cheque. To pay the cheque to someone other than the customer would be conversion and if the account were debited the claim of the customer's who is the true owner, could not be gainsaid. It is appreciated that it may be argued that Hightown branch is paying Lowtown branch and is thus paying another bank; but payment of the cheque has taken place where Lowtown branch has paid the cash. It is then that the customer's mandate was honoured.

The second part of the question involves no such negligence or payment out of the ordinary course of business since the cheque was paid without conflicting with any crossing. The banker can claim his protection and debit the customer's account without having to establish the genuineness of the endorsement.

Where the shopkeeper has become the holder he may be a 'holder in due course' as he has given value in good faith and, presumably, comes within the requirements of section 29 of the Bills of Exchange Act. It thus appears that, even had the bank been warned of the theft and the cheque stopped, the drawer would have been liable to the shopkeeper. There is no question of any endorsement having been forged. We are told that the cheque was endorsed *by the customer*. There are no damages for conversion because the benefit of the cheque belongs to the shopkeeper.

6 : Cheques drawn on a former bank

Mr A, who is known to you, writes to your branch of the Lowtown Bank saying that he wishes you to 'take over all his banking business from Bloggs Bank Limited'.

You send him an authority addressed to Bloggs Bank Limited which reads 'Please transfer my account to Lowtown Bank Ltd., Smithtown'. Mr A signs and returns the authority and Bloggs Bank Ltd sends you a payment for the balance. Over the following two days Bloggs Bank forward to you cheques totalling £105 drawn on them and dated prior to the transfer of the account to you. These cheques are paid to the debit of the new account at your branch, but Mr A subsequently disputes your action saying you had not authority to pay them.

Discuss the position of the Lowtown Bank.

From a practical aspect it would seem logical that the Lowtown Bank should pay the cheques amounting to £105 and drawn by Mr A prior to the transfer of the account from Bloggs Bank Ltd. However, the cheques were drawn on Bloggs Bank and, as such, were an instruction to that bank *only* to pay the £105 from his account with them.

The transfer of Mr A's business did not in itself give authority to the Lowtown Bank to pay the outstanding cheques. Before doing so they should have obtained the express permission of their new customer to debit his account.

The simplest method of dealing with this problem would have been for the Lowtown Bank to have obtained a separate authority in writing from Mr A authorising payment of outstanding cheques issued on his previous bankers prior to the transfer. This instruction could have been taken at the same time as the original authority for the transfer of the account.

Alternatively, the Lowtown Bank could have arranged with Mr A to ascertain what cheques were outstanding and to leave £105 on his account at Bloggs Bank to await their presentation, and the balance above this figure transferred.

The first method would seem less cumbersome.

24

The main risk in the Lowtown Bank paying these cheques without the permission of Mr A is the possibility that he may have counter-manded payment at Bloggs Bank. The stop instruction would not necessarily have been passed on to the Lowtown Bank upon transfer of the account.

In conclusion, Mr A is quite right in his assumption that the Low-town Bank had no authority to pay these cheques. However, if the debts represented by the cheques still existed there would seem to be no problem; although Mr A may have a case against the Bank there seems little point in any action being taken by the customer. If necessary, the bank could always stand in subrogation of the payees of the cheques.

If the cheques had been stopped at Bloggs Bank then the Lowtown Bank would have to refund the £105 to Mr. A. In this instance it would be possible however to try to obtain repayment from the payees, but any success would depend upon the nature of the dispute between Mr A and the payees.

There is one further point that may afford a legal defence, although in practice it would be unlikely to be taken up unless the figures were large. As the cheque is not drawn on the bank by which it is 'paid', that bank may be said to have negotiated the cheque in that it has given value for it. Whether or not these circumstances would entitle the bank to claim from the drawer and thus offset the latter's claim will in part be dependent upon whether the cheque is fully negotiable. In any event this may not be a successful ploy, but it could provide an answer for the bank. If the cheque had been stopped then the bank which 'paid' the cheque would probably be forced back on to its rights of subrogation.

7 : A benevolent society mandate

*The account of a benevolent society is operated by three signatories.
A member of the society calls on their bankers with a complaint that
all three signatories have resigned from the society as a result of a
misunderstanding, taking away with them the society's cheque book
and other papers relating to the account. They are also threatening to
form a rival society in the same name to give them the right to the
account. This allegation is confirmed. Meanwhile a cheque is presented
over the counter signed by the three persons.*

(a) What steps should the bank take?

*(b) Advise the society as to how the mandate of the three persons can
be revoked.*

The key to this situation hinges, apparently, on who exactly is the
bank's customer. This is, of course, the society and thus, indirectly,
the members of the society; and it is towards the society and its members that the bank's duty lies.

On the opening of the account, the bank will have taken its usual
form of mandate governing the operation of a club or society account.
This mandate will have been in the form of a resolution passed by
the society's committee or other governing body and would be expected
to cover the following points :

(1) That an account be opened with the bank in the name of the
society.

(2) That the bank be authorised to debit to the account, being in
credit, overdrawn or becoming overdrawn in consequence, cheques
and other instrument drawn on behalf of the society, provided these
are signed by the appropriate number of officials, *e.g.*, secretary and
treasurer, any two members of the committee, the chairman and one
committee member, *etc.*

(3) That the bank be supplied with a copy of the rules of the society.

(4) That the bank be furnished with the full names and specimen
signatures of the secretary, chairman, treasurer, and members of the
committee.

26

(5) That the above resolutions should remain in force until amended by notice in writing to the bank signed by the secretary.

(6) That the above resolution was a true copy of the appropriate entry in the society's minute book.

Then usually would follow a schedule of the full names, capacities and specimen signatures of those authorised to sign on the account and the completed document would be signed by the chairman and secretary.

The bank must be careful what action is taken on receipt of the member's complaint since this amounts to hearsay and could itself be the result of a misunderstanding. To ignore it, however, may prejudice the bank's position in any possible legal action resulting.

Inevitably the steps taken by the bank will be dependent upon their view as to the accuracy of the information given to them by the member who was called upon. First in relation to testing the statement it has to be borne in mind that it is alleged that the three signatories have re-signed. If in fact they have resigned then in all probability their power to operate the account has terminated. It does not seem from the question that there is any dispute as to whether or not the three persons had resigned. No banker would accept the oral intimation of a fourth member of the society, who may be genuinely misinterpreting the position or may be acting on mere hearsay. Thus the first step would be to verify the information. In the normal form of mandate the authority to sign on a benevolent society account would not be for Smith, or Jones or Robinson to do so as Smith, Jones or Robinson, but as officials of the society. Thus upon that basis one might contemplate returning a cheque, if the resignation has been confirmed, 'the drawer's signature requires confirmation'. It has to be remembered that a benevolent society is a particular form of friendly society and will come within the jurisdiction of the Registrar of Friendly Societies. If there is undoubted evidence as to the fact that the resignation has taken place then one need not pursue the position further; on the other hand if there is doubt then one should seek confirmation from the Registrar. In fact there will always be guidance. Again one has to realise that the nature of any cheque presented may affect the position. If, for example, there was an attempt to transfer the balance or a substantial part of the balance to another bank, even in the name or purporting to be in the name of the society, then confirmation should be sought. On the other hand, if the payments concerned under the old signatories are merely those of weekly grants – as evidenced from the history of the account – to a number of individuals, one would be hesitant to dishonour the cheques.

27

In fact in practice if the resignations had been simply routine a banker should have attempted from a practical standpoint to seek authority for payment rather than cause embarrassment· Most societies that operate as benevolent societies are likely to have brought themselves within the category of the friendly societies' legislation because of certain practical advantages. They can make large distributions, but are not subject to the restrictions placed upon a number of other kinds of charity.

As regards the threat to form a rival society in the same name in order to obtain the right to the account, it is difficult to see from the practical point of view how this could be achieved, since the bank would not act on any instructions to dispose of the balance of the account which it was not satisfied were duly authorised instructions. Also assuming the society was one which, by its rules, was registered with the Registrar of Friendly Societies, it would be as well if the society, or indeed the bank, informed that official of the present circumstances. Such circumstances may possibly also have been covered in the society's rules and, as mentioned earlier, the bank would probably have a copy of these rules which could be of additional guidance.

8 : A garnishee order and uncleared effects

West-town Bank is served on 4 April with a garnishee order nisi on its account, A. Smith Esq. The garnishee order was dated the same day, 4 April, and covered an amount up to £5,000. The bank stopped Mr Smith's account and advised the court of the credit balance of £4,000.

Unfortunately the balance was not cleared and on 5 April a cheque for £1,000 was returned unpaid marked 'refer to drawer' making only a cleared balance of £3,000.

Advise the bank.

When a person is subject to garnishee proceedings it does not necessarily mean that he is an unsatisfactory customer of the bank, although this may often be the case. A garnishee order nisi emanates from the High Court attaching either all debts due from the bank to the customer, or all debts so due not exceeding a specified amount, pending a decision of the matter on a date set in the order. *Only those debts are attached which are due to the customer by the bank at the actual time of the service of the garnishee nisi.* Any uncleared cheques in course of collection therefore cannot be regarded as coming within this category of debts actually due to the customer – these must be disregarded in arriving at the balance which is to be attached.

When a garnishee order is received it is essential that the bank is able to identify beyond any reasonable doubt which account is attached – if there is any doubt whatsoever no action should be taken pending clarification of the position.

In the problem we are told that the balance of Mr Smith's account totalling £4,000, was uncleared and therefore was not subject to attachment under the garnishee order. The judgment creditor's solicitors should have been advised on 4 April by the West-town Bank that there were no debts due to Mr Smith from the bank at the time of service of the order. The bank should also have informed Mr Smith of receipt of the order and the action taken by them. It is customary in a case of this nature where uncleared items form part of the customer's balance to open a new account and transfer the amount of uncleareds to it, the customer being informed that this has been done. However, in this instance all the balance was uncleared and no useful purpose would have been served in adopting this procedure.

At one time it is true that the case of *Jones* v. *Coventry* (1909) decided that items credited as cash were available for a garnishee order. Since that time, however, the view has been altered by the decision in *Underwood* v. *Barclays Bank, Ltd.* (1924). Perhaps the best view is the summary given by Mr John Tonkyn in the *Journal of the Institute of Bankers,* vol. LXXV, December 1954, p. 340 :

Garnishee Orders and uncleared effects
In general, I should regard all uncleared effects as not attached by the order. The point is that there is no sum owing to the customer, at the time of service, in respect of the uncleared effects, nor can it be said that uncleared effects constitute a sum certainly accruing due. Even if I had occasionally paid cheques against uncleared effects, I should still maintain the same attitude. The only possible exception would be a case in which I had a definite understanding with the customer whereby he would be entitled to draw against uncleared effects, but arrangements sufficiently definite for this purpose would be unusual.

Even then there is considerable doubt as to whether the customer entitled to draw against uncleared effects would be subject to a garnishee order.

It is true that whenever a judgment is obtained and the judgment debtor has an asset there is some form of execution to enable a creditor to realise that asset. Where a person owns shares or has a share in a partnership, or has rights due under a contract, there is the process that is known as 'equitable execution' which enables a receiver to be appointed so that the benefit can be obtained for the judgment creditor (as distinct in due course from being distributed in bankruptcy to the creditors generally). Strictly, therefore, it may be suggested that the customer's right against the banker is contractual. In other words, once cheques are deposited the customer has a right to borrow from the banker against the security of the cheques. Probably that right could be pursued successfully by a judgment creditor theoretically by way of equitable execution because it is a contractual right. In practice this is not likely to be successful because of the short time in which a cheque takes to be collected. Furthermore the circumstances giving rise to the garnishee order may of themselves justify the banker in declining to go ahead with the arrangement made for the customer to borrow against uncleared effects. That is to say that if a facility is made available to a customer without the knowledge that judgment debts are outstanding against that customer, the knowledge of the existence of such judgment debts may well justify the facility being withdrawn.

All the above is somewhat academic, but feasibly represents the true legal basis. The answer to the question, therefore, is that, as mentioned by the winning correspondent, as there was no cleared balance there were no funds available for the judgment creditor and the bank should endeavour to submit a further affidavit. It is unlikely that damages to the judgment creditor could ensue, although it is just possible, through his being unable to attach another asset owing to the delay occasioned by the bank's incorrect statement.

9 : Appointment of receiver and late returns

On a Saturday morning Anytown Bank Ltd. receives amongst the clearing cheques drawn by one of its company customers. There is a substantial credit balance on the account; but, due to pressure of work, the bank staff are unable to examine the cheques in the clearing on the day they were received. On the following Monday, at 9.55 a.m., the bank manager is informed by the company's managing director that a receiver was appointed by a debenture holder on the previous Friday and the former tells the latter that he is unable to pay cheques drawn on the company's account without the authority of the receiver. The former tries to contact the receiver concerning the cheques received on Saturday but is unable to do so by 12 noon.

Should the bank pay the cheques received on Saturday or not? (Although banks no longer open on Saturdays the problem has been included because the principle is applicable to other days of the week).

The powers of a receiver are derived from Section 109 of the Law of Property Act, 1925 and from the document creating the charge. He is frequently appointed while an action in which there is any question as to property of any kind is pending, such as under a specific power contained in a debenture or debenture trust deed or more often, where a company defaults. When he is appointed, whether by the court or not, he has power to take possession, to carry on the business, to sell, lease or let the property, to make arrangements or compromises or to call up any uncalled capital. He has very wide powers for he, at once, takes possession of the undertaking of the company and assumes complete control of it, to the exclusion of the powers of the directors and of the claims of all other creditors except those of certain preferential creditors. According to Lord Atkinson in *Moss S.S. Co.* v. *Whinney* (1912) AC 254, the

. . . appointment of a receiver and manager over the assets and business of a company does not dissolve or annihilate the company, any more than the taking of possession by the mortgagee of the fee of land let to tenants annihilates the mortgagor. Both continue to exist; but it entirely supersedes the company in the conduct of its business, deprives it of all power to enter into contracts in relation to that business, or to sell, pledge, or otherwise dispose of the property put into the possession or under the control of the receiver and manager. Its power in these respects are entirely in abeyance.

Having obtained such control it becomes a question for the consideration of the receiver as to what course should be followed. In some cases he will decide to carry on the business for a time with a prospect of selling it as a going concern; or if he considers against it and that the business is valueless as a going concern, then he will stop the business and realise the assets."

The result of appointing a receiver is to crystallise the security, to prevent the company from dealing with its assets and to vest the control of them for the time being in the receiver. A receiver *appointed by the court* is an officer of the court and the court will see that he carries out any contracts made by him as receiver, and any interference with him is a contempt of court. Lord Haldane in *Parsons* v. *Sovereign Bank of Canada* (1913) quoted that the court receiver

. . . is the agent neither of the debenture holders, whose credit he cannot pledge, nor of the company who cannot control him. He is an officer of the court put in to discharge certain duties described by the order appointing him . . . The company remains in existence, but it has lost its title to control its assets and affairs."

A receiver appointed under a mortgage is not the agent of the mortgagee who appoints him but of the mortgagor; and similarly under a debenture he is a receiver not only in respect of the particular debenture belonging to the man who appointed him but also for all the other debenture holders in the same series. After liquidation he is the agent of the debenture holders; and they may be liable on any contracts he makes. When appointed, he has to notify the company immediately of his appointment (Companies Act 1948, *s.*372). Furthermore by virtue of *s.*370, every invoice, order for goods or business letters issued by or on behalf of the company or the receiver, being a document on or in which the name of the company appears, has to contain a statement that a receiver has been appointed and there are penalties for default.

Normally, a bank becomes aware of a company's financial difficulties and the appointment of a receiver is not a surprise (in some cases

33

C

he may have been appointed by the bank) but the actual date of his appointment may not be known to the bank until a few days later. Certain it is that the bank should know of all charges created by a company over its property as they must be registered within 21 days of the date upon which they are made, with the Registrar of Companies (s.95, Companies Act 1948). So, the signatories upon the cheques presented on Saturday are unauthorised, as the receiver is now in control of the company and the company's account must be stopped, and in due course the bank may have to pay over the credit balance to the receiver. There is no principle by which the amount of cheques may be recovered if paid before notice is received by the bank, nor are there any legal cases to give guidance. The bank would naturally want evidence of the appointment of the receiver but that may be after cheques had been paid. It may be that as in the case of *Re A. Boynton, Ltd.* (1910) that if the bank pays the cheques and they are subsequently disallowed the bank account could possibly be overdrawn thereby and it could be an 'outside' creditor when its claim must rank behind the debenture holders costs and the receiver's remuneration. The receiver is bound to pay the preferential creditors first and if insufficient funds they are proportionally paid. The bank is not to know what transactions are covered by the cheques in question, and if they are not preferential payments they could be in question. Even if they are preferential payments, and the receiver pays proportional preferential payment, the bank might still be in difficulties.

By the Rules of the Committee of London Clearing Bankers, cheques received through the London clearing may be returned up to noon of the day following receipt, but on the second day, if return is contemplated, it is bank custom to phone the presenting bank of the dishonoured cheque. There is no specific provision in the Bills of Exchange Act 1882 which prescribes the period available to the drawee bank for deciding whether to pay or dishonour cheques. However, if the above rules are observed, such action could not be attacked; conversely if the rules are not observed and the cheque is returned after the stipulated period, objection could properly be taken (*Parr's Bank, Ltd.* v. *Thomas Ashby & Co.* 1898). Following this is the case of *The Royal Bank of Ireland, Ltd.* v. *O'Rourke* (1962), a decision of the Supreme Court of Ireland in which the court alluded to s.45 of the Bills of Exchange Act as to presenting a cheque within reasonable time, and s. 48 (12) as to giving notice of dishonour within reasonable time (otherwise the endorser is discharged). The court continued that the duty of the paying banker is to deal with a cheque within such time as is reasonable; regard should be had to the nature of the bill, the usage of trade with regard to similar bills, and the facts of the particular case. Unfortunately, the judgment, while deciding in that case that the defence that the cheque had not been presented within a reasonable time failed, it did not decide the question of what is unreasonable delay; and it is still a question of doubt. On the other hand, the presenter of the cheque is entitled to know as soon as possible whether a cheque is paid or not and is entitled to assume that after the normal period of clearance, a cheque is paid if not returned. So, if a bank refuses to pay or return a cheque, it may have a liability on the basis that payment has been presumed·

From a purely practical aspect the bank could telephone the presenting bankers that the cheques are being returned because of the appointment of a receiver. Between noon and the end of the business day the bank should endeavour to contact the receiver. The cheques should be returned and early on Tuesday morning efforts should be made to acquaint the receiver of the position; and if the cheques are to be paid the collecting banker could be notified accordingly. From this outlook, if the bank should have paid the cheques he may be liable but there is a legal doubt; whereas if he returns them, then they can be subsequently paid, or better still, the receiver can pay them, as it does not necessarily mean that the company will become insolvent.

There are, here, two points of legal controversy :

(i) Whether the Clearing House Rules bind both the customers and the bank, or whether they bind only the customer and are available principally for the convenience of bankers, and,

(ii) the circumstances in which a late return can be made.

On the first point, the view in Paget is that they do not necessarily give customers any rights, although this is open to argument because it would seem to be inequitable and perhaps illogical that the customers could have the burden but not the benefit of implied terms of the banker/customer contract. On the second aspect it appears that *strictly speaking* a cheque presented on the Saturday can only be returned on the Monday if the delay is due to inadvertence or pressure of work. These terms may be associated with computer banking, but it would be very difficult for anyone to dispute a banker's contention that he came within the classifications.

So, in conclusion, the paying banker is unlikely to be vulnerable because if the late return is not possible he can rely on the lateness of the notice of the appointment of the receiver. It has not at any time been held that a banker is liable if he has no notice of the appointment of a receiver under a debenture or mortgage, as distinct from where a receiving order has been made in bankruptcy proceedings. The latter, of course, operates from the beginning of the day on which it is made; this, however, is a direct consequence of a statute. There are parallels – in, for example, that it is notice of death – not death – that terminates the authority of a banker to pay cheques.

Part two : The collecting banker

The position of the collecting banker, in one sense like the paying banker, can also be considered from two aspects. In the one instance the collecting banker is an agent. He must do what his principal tells him and he must do it expeditiously. If he acts without normal skill or delays he may be responsible for any loss ensuing to his customer. On the other hand, sometimes the cheque that he receives for collection is, quite unbeknown to the banker, the property of a third party. Normally, but for the statutory protection, he would be liable for conversion. This is an action that can be brought at law in respect of any inter-meddling, whether innocent or otherwise, by a third party with property belonging to a particular person. In this case the cheque may really belong to X and the banker may be asked to credit it to the account of his customer AB. Then, but for the statutory protection now contained in Section 4 of the Cheques Act and applying to a variety of documents as well as cheques, the banker would be vulnerable for this action for conversion.

Sometimes where a banker has lent to a customer or has paid against uncleared effects, the banker himself may be regarded as having become the transferee of the cheque, and have the rights against the drawer of the cheque, despite the fact that the cheque is stopped. This is considered in the ensuing chapter on bills and negotiation of cheques.

As to the specific questions :

Question 1
Delay speaks for itself. The use of the Clearing House is undoubtedly authorised. Whether the customer can claim rights if the rules are disregarded is open to some doubt as may be seen from question 7 in this section and also the note on Question 9 on page 13.

Question 2
All banking students are aware of the rules that have grown up governing the taking of references. Subsequently the banker's position has been improved by the decision in *Marfani* v. *Midland Bank Ltd.* (1968 2 A.E.R. 573).

Question 3

The collection of a cheque for a solicitor's clients account depends upon its particular nature and is not necessarily applicable to other so-called clients accounts.

Question 4

The measure of enquiry on the collection of third party cheques is more and more becoming a matter of the practice of banking so long as the particular transaction is not in itself obviously negligent on the part of the banker. It is true, however, that in *Baker* v. *Barclays Bank Ltd.* 1955 2 A.E.R. 571 Devlin J. (as he then was) said that a bank manager was on enquiry when he saw "large" (?) cheques frequently endorsed over to third parties.

Question 5

Where, of course, the customer is undoubted financially then the banker as that customer's agent can always look to the customer should any claim arise. The facts described in the problem are, however, unusual.

Question 6

This is a straightforward indication of the need for the banker to have the statutory protection. The legal background is instructive. The point was before the court recently in *Kenton* v. *Barclays Bank* (Current Law 1977).

Question 7

The point here involves the use of the Clearing House and in many ways is one of the most probing questions in the volume. Also see question 9 on page 13.

Question 8

The answer is discursive and interesting *but* the note in the last paragraph almost certainly represents the law as it stands today. The Banking Act 1979 Section 47 now gives proportionate relief to a banker collecting a cheque who has been negligent if the plaintiff himself has also been negligent.

1 : Delay in collecting a cheque

On Monday, a cheque for £10,000, was drawn by a customer of a branch bank, in favour of another customer of that branch, is paid into his account by the payee. In answer to his enquiry, he is told that the cheque is paid. Unfortunately, due to an error in the day's sorting, the cheque is not debited to the drawer's account but is dispatched in the day's remittances and so is presented once again to the branch in Wednesday morning's clearing. In the meantime, on Tuesday, the drawer of the cheque has died and the bank has failed to notice that the £10,000 has not at that time been debited to his account. What should the bank do on the second presentation of the cheque and would the position be different if the payee had not been told that the cheque was paid?

The circumstances of this question are sufficiently unusual for one to think that the incident in fact happened. At first glance there is the thought that somewhat similar events might have occurred in practice without there having been the slightest suggestion that the bank could not remedy its mistake. The cheque might have been debited to the wrong account or have been lost within the branch for a day or so; yet in practice, and probably in law also, there would have appeared to have been no reason for doing anything other than passing the entry to the debit of the account on which it had been drawn 'as at' the day when the payee had been told that the cheque was paid. There is no point in seeking to disguise what has happened. The fact that the cheque left the confines of the branch would not alter the position unless payment had been refused.

On the other hand the problem raises a number of aspects that are of more legal and practical importance than one would at first think. There is the perennial topic of the enquiry by the customer of the same branch as to whether a cheque drawn by another customer of the same branch will be paid. There is also the less usual question of when 'payment' is in law effected. Finally there is the associated problem of how long a banker has to decide whether or not payment is to be made.

On the first point, as to whether an answer can be demanded by a customer of the branch (or perhaps of another branch) there is the standard solution contained in *Questions on Banking Practice* (No. 432, 10th ed.) that

(432) If a cheque is sent by post by the collecting banker direct to the drawee banker, with a request to pay over the amount through the head offices of the two banks (or, if there is an account between the banks, to credit the account), within what time must the drawee banker return the cheque, if he is unable to pay it?

Answer: Not later than the day after receipt. In such circumstances the drawee banker receives the cheque as agent for presentation to himself (see Paget, 7th ed., p. 435), and so has the same time for giving notice of dishonour to his principal, the collecting banker, as if he, the drawee banker, were himself the holder of the cheque (sec. 49(13) of the Bills of Exchange Act), namely, until the day after dishonour (under sub-sec. (12) of that section).

Usually the cheque will be returned on the day of receipt. This is undoubtedly a satisfactory line to adopt in practice. In addition however there is the arrangement of the special presentation. In *Turner* v. *London & Provincial Bank Ltd.* 1903 (*Legal Decision Affecting Banking,* vol.II p. 33) evidence was given that it was common practice for banks to make special presentations, although it was mainly a matter for the banker's discretion. One might conclude perhaps that a customer has a 'right' to this service only occasionally (if at all) since obviously a too frequent indulgence of its nature could dislocate banking business as a whole. In this context the facility can hardly be denied occasionally merely because the cheque is drawn on the same branch as that where the holder keeps his account. Subject to this reservation the customer must wait till the close of business. Yet the practice of affirming readily that payment will be made where the point is beyond doubt may give rise to a contrary innuendo where unlike previous occasions the banker hesitates, but so long as his hesitation were justified he would have nothing to fear.

In law payment need not be made by the transfer of money. In *Meyer* v. *Sze Hai Tong Banking & Insurance Co.* (1913) AC 847 it was held that payment was effected by the delivery to the presenter of a draft drawn by the paying banker. Similarly when there is a commitment to pay within the banker-customer contract then in the normal course of events that payment may and must be implemented. Whether payment is effected at the time of commitment or later does not alter the fact that the customer's account may be charged.

Finally there is the third aspect as to whether the banker has to pay on demand. The terms by definition of a cheque – are that payment has to be made on demand. This can be varied by Clearing House rules or other implied (or express) arrangements between banker and customer. Presentation over the counter of an open cheque (or it seems by another banker of a crossed cheque specially presented) necessitates an answer immediately. The position is subject to the right of the banker to make further enquiries when there is embarrassment – such as may arise from oriental characters or when the likelihood of the person tendering an open cheque being entitled is almost out of the question. (Compare the instance given by Mr Justice Wright in the case of *Auchteroni* v. *Midland Bank* (1928 2 K.B.294) of the unshaven tramp presenting the open cheque for £1,000).

Thus the bank debits the cheque as of the date of presentation. Even if the payee had not been told it appears that the paying banker would be in difficulty if he did otherwise – since apart from other aspects he would have to explain a late return *and the presenter could presume payment*. Whereas to pay gives no embarrassment unless the customer's executor has been informed of the balance. Then only in the very remote event of his having acted on the information to the detriment of the estate, such as by having sold stocks at a depreciated price would there be any possibility of a successful claim against the bank.

2 : Fraudulent reference as to customer's identity

Miss M. Smith has a current account at the Westown Bank Limited which has been satisfactorily administered for a number of years. When the account was opened a reference was taken to which the reply was satisfactory and the referee's banker confirmed that the referee was a suitable person to give a reference.

On 31 May 1966 Miss Smith calls at her bank to say that she is now married and that she wishes her account title to be amended to Mrs M. Brown. It is not the Westown Bank's practice to ask to see a Marriage Certificate and the original reference is regarded as sufficient for the account to be continued in the new name.

Miss Smith is not, in fact, married but is employed by a Mrs M. Brown as a part-time cleaner from whom she had stolen a number of cheques payable to Mrs M. Brown. These she pays into her newly-styled bank account for collection, and in due course withdraws the money and disappears.

The thefts are subsequently discovered and Mrs Brown sues the bank. What is the bank's position?

The answer to this problem depends whether the Westown Bank Ltd. as a collecting banker has been negligent. If the bank has not been negligent then it is protected by Section 4 of the Cheques Act from the consequences of a conversion of the cheque. If it is not so protected, then it is liable to Mrs Brown. Cheques belonging to Mrs Brown were collected and the proceeds made available to Miss M. Smith. This is in law a conversion, although the bank, is, of course, quite innocent in that it was unaware of what was happening. Nevertheless a legal liability arises in the same way as if someone is handed an article to look after and by mistake returns it incorrectly to a third party. There has been a conversion and the person concerned is liable for damages. The bank would escape that liability only if it can bring itself within Section 4 of the Cheques Act 1957, which among other requirements indicates that it must not have been negligent. Whether a bank has been negligent or not depends on circumstances. Sometimes an act of a bank is of its nature negligent. It is not enough to say that other banks do the same thing. For example, in the case of *Lloyds Bank Ltd.* v. *Savory & Co.* (1933) A.C. 201, it was of no avail to the bank to establish that other banks, like Lloyds, took a different attitude merely because a third party cheque was paid in at a branch *other than* where the account was kept. The events amounted to negligence. On the other hand it has been several times indicated by the courts that negligence depends on the practice of bankers. Where, for example, it is a question of whether having regard to particular circumstances enquiries should be made or whether enquiries that have been made have been answered reasonably satisfactorily, then the attitude of other bankers, or more specifically of other bank managers, will be material and probably conclusive. It is very difficult for a court in the face of evidence from, say, two or three other banks' managers saying that they would have acted in the same way as the bank manager concerned in the case, to hold that there has been negligence, unless the situation is one in which the particular act speaks for itself.

Turning to the question as to whether Westown Bank has been negligent, one may reasonably look to the practice of bankers. We are told in the question that it is not the Westown Bank's practice to see a Marriage Certificate and that they rely on the original reference. It is true that the negligence is not in relation to opening the account, but negligence is not regarded as associated solely with the collection of any particular cheque; as was indicated in *Motor Guarantee Corporation Ltd.* v. *Midland Bank Ltd.* (1937) 4 A.E.R. 90, the history of the account was indicated as being relevant. If, therefore, bankers generally in the circumstances indicated in the question make a practice of obtaining a sight of the Marriage Certificate, then it will be difficult for Westown Bank Ltd. to defend a claim of Mrs Brown. The practice may vary, but it is known that some banks do habitually ask for such evidence. There is also the possible indication of the attitude in the following question and answer from the Institute of Bankers' *Questions on Banking Practice:*

192. What signature should a married woman use in withdrawing money deposited by her before marriage in her maiden name?

Answer: If the bank is satisfied as to her identity there is no reason why she should not sign her married name.

This is not conclusive of practice and, of course, relates to a security. The implication is that if there is doubt as to identification evidence should be sought.

Thus, in all probability, Mrs Brown would succeed in claiming from Westown Bank. It is not necessarily the Marriage Certificate that is material. It is a question of identity. Often where unmarried parties are co-habiting the lady will take the name of 'Mrs X' for the sake of appearances. The Bank will recognise the possibility of her appropriating the cheques of the other Mrs X (or there may be more than one other ! !).

3 : Collecting a cheque payable to a solicitor's client

A firm of solicitors, Messrs Y & Y, are valued customers of North-town Bank, Blackacre. They pay in for the credit of their clients account a cheque for £5,000 drawn by the Blackacre Building Society Ltd on Southtown Bank, Blackacre. The cheque is payable to 'Joe Soap per Messrs X & Y' and is not endorsed.

Messrs X & Y tell Northtown Bank that a completion is due that afternoon and that they want the cheque cleared specially. Can North-town Bank comply and credit X & Y's account? Joe Soap is unknown to Northtown Bank and lives out of town and cannot be approached or his endorsement obtained. What are the legal and practical risks?

The crux of this question is whether the bank would be in order in accepting the cheque payable to 'Joe Soap per Messrs X & Y' for the credit of the latter's account without the endorsement of Joe Soap.

In ordinary circumstances, the bank would be negligent if they took the cheque for credit of Messrs X & Y without Joe Soap's endorsement and would lose the protection given to collecting bankers in Section 4 of the Cheques Act, 1957, through acting negligently.

However, solicitors' accounts are an exception to the general rule and an examination of the Solicitors Act, 1957* and the statutory rules and orders made under the authority of the Act is necessary. Relevant extracts concerning this situation are as follows:

Rule 5 (b). Where a solicitor holds or receives a cheque or draft which includes client's money or trust money of one or more trusts, if he does not split the cheque or draft, he shall, if any part thereof consists of client's money, and may, in any other case, pay the cheque or, draft into a client account.

Rule 3 (Extract). Every solicitor who receives client's money is permitted and elects to pay into a client's account, shall without delay pay such money into a client's account. Any solicitor may keep one client account or as many such accounts as he thinks fit.

Section 85 (1). Relieves the banker of enquiring whether every transaction on a solicitor's account is in accordance with the rules:

45

'Subject to the provisions of this section no bank shall, in connection with any transaction on account of any solicitor kept with it or with any other bank (other than an account kept by a solicitor as trustee for a specified beneficiary) incur any liability or be under any obligation to make any enquiry or be deemed to have knowledge of any right of any person to any money paid or credited to any such account, which it would not incur or be under or be deemed to have in the case of an account kept by a person entitled absolutely to all the money paid or credited to it :

Provided that nothing in this subsection shall relieve a bank from any liability or obligation under which it would be apart from section twenty-nine of this Act or this section'.

A solicitor's clients account is like a 'bare' trusteeship, money is being held in trust for the client until such time as the solicitor is required to pay it over to him or to another party on his behalf.

Therefore, if a bank is satisfied that there is a genuine solicitor/client relationship and they would not normally doubt the solicitor's word, any cheques made payable to the client may be paid into the solicitor's *Clients Account* without the client's endorsement. The bank would not be negligent in collecting such cheques.

In the case in question, the payee is already evidence that there is a solicitor/client relationship; furthermore, it is stated that it is in connection with the purchase of a property. The cheque can then safely be accepted for the credit of Messrs X & Y's clients account without the endorsement of Joe Soap.

The cheque may then be specially presented to the Southdown Bank who being the paying banker will be protected by Section 1 of the Cheques Act, 1957, for the absence of any endorsement.

It is perhaps appropriate to mention that the answer does not directly conflict with the Memorandum issued by the Committee of London Clearing Bankers on 23 September 1957, and that, although the case of *Slingsby* v. *Westminster Bank Ltd.* (1932) 1 K.B. 544 decided that a cheque so drawn required an endorsement indicating its vicarious nature, this position may well be regarded as having been affected by the impact of the Solicitors Act quoted above. In the event of difficulty the bank can of course look to the solicitors who will normally be 'quite undoubted' for the figure mentioned in the question.

* The Rules made under the 1974 Act are to similar effect.

46

4 : Collecting a third party cheque

*A messenger from your customer X Y Z Ltd pays in a credit on their
behalf included in which is a cheque payable to 'J. Smith', The A. B.
Co. Ltd.' and endorsed 'J. Smith'. The messenger is only able to tell
you that J. Smith is a commercial traveller with The A. B. Co. Ltd.
and there is no-one at your customer's office able to give further information.*

*Should you accept this cheque for the credit of your customer's
account and if so what would be your bank's position should it subsequently transpire that J. Smith has been defrauding his employers
and that the latter are claiming negligence on the part of the bank in
accepting the cheque.*

The first question that occurs or should occur to a banker when he is
considering a potential loss consequent upon his collecting a particular
third party cheque is the standing of his customer. Apart from the
special instance mentioned later in this answer, if the customer who
receives the money is undoubted for the amount of the cheque the
banker runs no risk in that he can look to the customer in relation to
any claim. In the question the account being credited is that of XYZ
Ltd. If that company is substantial and has received the benefit of
the amount collected, then, if there is a claim for conversion against the
bank, reimbursement of such claim can be obtained from the customer. In fact it is usually open to the claimant to sue the customer who
receives the money as an alternative to suing the banker. This may
happen because a banker has often the answer that he has not been
negligent and can therefore rely upon Section 4 of the Cheques Act
1957. At all events the third party will claim from the customer direct
because he, as distinct from the banker, has no statutory protection
that he can call to his aid (or at least use to provide a further point of
defence that has to be argued).

Where, however, the customer is not strong enough to withstand
the debit the banker is concerned that he shall not be regarded as
having been negligent. In general, negligence depends on the practice
of bankers, unless the facts in their nature quite evidently reflect negli-

47

gence. Whether, for example, the answer received to an enquiry that is pursued should be regarded by a banker as adequate in relation to the collection of a third party cheque may well depend upon the views, in all the circumstances, that would be taken by managers of other banks, whose evidence may in some instances be of assistance. In the present instance, upon the thought that the customer may not be good for the amount, the questions are : what enquiries should be made and whether the replies should be accepted. The answer made in relation to the cheque payable to J. Smith, The A.B. Co. Ltd, endorsed by Smith, was simply that the messenger from XYZ Ltd knew that Smith was a traveller for the A.B. Co. Ltd. Generally one might conclude that anyone writing a cheque in favour of Smith adding the name of his employers might wish the money to reach the employers through Smith. There is certainly ambiguity which in a third party cheque would be likely to be considered sufficient to warrant enquiry. The answer that Smith as a traveller and an employee of The A.B. Co. Ltd. is hardly reassuring especially as, upon any view, the cheque is a third party cheque. In addition, unless it can be suggested that the bank need not concern itself with the regularity of an endorsement, which seems however to be the true position, the endorsement (on the basis of *Slingsby* v. *District Bank* (1932 1.K.B. 544) of Smith alone may well be irregular and thus an additional source of evidence of negligence on part of the bank. In the Slingsby case the cheque was payable 'per Cumberbirch and Potts' as distinct from the example where the name of the employee is added to that of Smith. Thus one would think that enquiry was necessary and the answer insufficient, in which event the bank would be vulnerable in so far as the customer may not be able to reimburse the bank with the amount.

There is a further point generally as to negligence in relation to the collection of a third party cheque. The banker has a contractual duty to his customer. If, for example, he receives a series of third party cheques and credits them to that customer's account at the behest of the customer's clerk it may be that the failure to mention the matter to the customer will enable the clerk to carry out an internal fraud by manipulating the customer's book keeping. In that event it is just possible that there could be a claim for negligence in performing the contract of banker and customer. This was the basis of a claim in an Australian case that came before the Privy Council : *Universal Guarantee Property Co. Ltd.* v. *National Bank of Australasia* (1965 2. A.E.R. 98). In that case the bank was held not to have been negligent on the particular facts despite the cheques paid in having been *drawn by* the customers payable to third parties. However, the type of claim cannot be ruled out for the future, even although the cheques are credited to the customer's account.

To summarise (*a*) the banker normally has no risk if the customer is undoubted for the amount of the cheque involved; (*b*) the circumstances may well amount to negligence and cause the banker to lose his statutory protection against conversion if he needed it because his customer could not meet the amount of the claim; and (*c*) there is a possible exception to (*a*) if the omission to raise the matter permits a fraud that might otherwise be revealed.

D

5 : The customer's responsibility for cheques collected for his account

The XYZ Company issued a cheque for £20 16s 5d to B who alleged that he had never received it. In due course the XYZ Company wrote to B telling him that the cheque had been paid by their bankers and had passed through the Southdown Bank. As it happened, B had a small deposit account at the Southdown Bank, and he called to see the manaager to ask for his advice. On checking the records at the Southdown Bank the manager discovered that the cheque had been received for the credit of good customer C. (1) What is the position of the Southdown Bank in respect of its good customer C? and (2) What practical steps can be taken to assist customer B?

The circumstances of the above problem are somewhat unusual. In particular there the coincidence that B, who has enquired from the Southdown Bank because the cheque was collected through that bank, also himself has a deposit account there. It is proposed to look at the problem primarily from the standpoint of the Southdown Bank and then deal chronologically with what they would be advised to do.

The thought that is likely to occur first to the manager of the Southdown Bank is whether there has been a mistake or dishonesty. His good customer C is not only of honest reputation but also can personally be ruled out in that the amount is relatively small. He could have cashed the cheque for a third party who may himself be innocent, such as the member of his staff or he, C, may have been in direct contact with someone who stole the cheque. That there was a mistake is perhaps less likely, but cheques have been known to be paid-in in error quite innocently by a recipient to whom they have been wrongly addressed. B, we are told in the question, alleges that he has never received the cheque. The manager presumably knows less of B but must conclude that it is highly improbable that B, even if not honest, would have the temerity and audacity to claim £20 fraudulently when he knows that enquiries are likely to elucidate the history of the matter. The manager has every right *vis-à-vis* B to disclose the matter to C. The manager knows that the bank has no risk of loss because if there had been a confusion he can insist that C's account is debited. He will therefore approach C having in mind that C may have to face a loss if he has cashed the cheque for a third party who is not entitled. This is because C will be liable for conversion to the true owner of the cheque (either the XYZ Co. or B – as to which, see below). It is, of course, only a banker who can claim statutory protection. Whatever the bank manager learns he will tell B, no doubt with the concurrence of C, but unless the circumstances were very peculiar – such as B being involved in fraud – C could not object to such disclosure.

The position of B will depend on what has happened. Incidentally any comment given to B on his position by the manager of the Southdown Bank should be on the basis that they are without responsibility. It can hardly be suggested that current banking advertisements, however big-hearted, offer their customers free legal advice involving responsibility. B's rights *vis-à-vis* the XYZ Co. will depend upon his relationship with the company. If the cheque has never reached B then, *prima facia,* the Post Office is at fault and the Post Office is deemed to be the agent of the sender except, as is the position in the majority of cases, if the sender has the express or implied authority of the recipient to use the post; sometimes the latter position may be set up as a result of a course of dealing. The position of B will then be dependent on the relationship between XYZ Co. and himself. If the payment is as a result of an arrangement involving the despatch by post of the cheque to B or if B has asked that the cheque be sent to him, then the property in the cheque passes to B at the time of posting. There is quite a lineage of cases as to the Post Office as agent. If there is no such arrangement the property in the lost cheque is that of the XYZ Co. If the cheque is the property of the XYZ Co. B can demand payment of the obligation (assuming he has not received the cheque) and XYZ Co. can bring an action for conversion against any third party who has handled the cheque without their authority. If as more likely the Post Office was the agent of B, then it is B's property that is lost. Whilst there is a right to demand a duplicate cheque against an indemnity, if XYZ Co.'s account has been debited there is an obvious loss and obviously an immediate claim – so such a request would be pointless. B, however, can sue a third party who has handled the cheque even if the cheque was fully negotiable. As it needed endorsement for transfer, the forgery may prevent the intermeddler from claiming that he was a 'holder in due course' —the instrument being void because of the forgery. If the cheque had been bearer then any third party who was a 'holder in due course' could not be sued. To know where he stands in the light of the above comments, B must find out what happened.

6 : Conversion of a cheque obtained by a customer by fraud

A steals a car and sells it to a motor dealer who makes out a cheque in his favour for £300. A had some months previously opened a deposit account at the R Bank, in respect of which no references had been taken up at the time. At A's request the R Bank collects the cheque and A withdraws the proceeds. The motor dealer discovers the fraud and seeks to claim from the R Bank. What is their position? Would it have made any difference if the true name of A had been X?

Bankers may sometimes in practice obtain references where a deposit account is opened. Normally they do not expect to be asked to collect cheques for such an account, but if they do, and have not taken up references at the time the account was opened, then it is highly probable that their action will be regarded as negligence either by collecting the cheque exceptionally or because no references were taken when the account was opened. If the account is of such a nature that, exceptionally or otherwise, cheques are going to be collected for its credit then it is only reasonable that the same enquiries should be made as would normally be made on the opening of a current account. Remotely the banker may perhaps argue that if he had known the customer as a deposit account holder for a number of years the position is altered. However the question states that the account had been opened only a few months earlier. Thus the protection of Section 4 of the Cheques Act 1957 is lost. The banker cannot establish that he has collected the cheques 'without negligence'. He is then subject to an action for conversion. Conversion is the liability that any banker would have if he collected a cheque for a customer who had no title to it, apart from the protection given by the Cheques Act. It is, strictly speaking, the wrongful interference with goods of another inconsistent with the rights of possession of that other person. When a cheque is converted there is the same event, the cheque being regarded by a legal fiction as a chattel having the value equivalent to the amount for which it is drawn. This point is made specifically by Scrutton, L.J., in *Lloyds Bank* v. *Chartered Bank of India* (1929 1.K.B. 40). Thus if there has been a conversion of the cheque the collecting banker is liable in that he has lost the protection afforded by the Cheques Act.

The most difficult question is whether there has been a conversion. This depends on whether the cheque was obtained, payable as we may presume to the customer, by a misrepresentation, other than, for example, an impersonation. It is well known that if someone is persuaded to sign a cheque, thinking it is a different instrument altogether, no property in the cheque passes. For a third party to deal with it is a conversion—it is the intermeddling with the property of the drawer. So clearly is the case where a cheque is obtained by impersonating a third party. There is then no intention of the drawer to pass the property in the cheque to the payee. Again, to deal with it is conversion of the drawer's property. However where the fraud stems from a different misrepresentation, as to ownership of a car, it is submitted that the position is different. The aspect is summarised in Paget's *Law of Banking*, 7th Edition, page 335, in the following terms :

A man is induced by fraud to execute and issue negotiable instrument, knowing its character, and there being no substitution of one person for another. The contract is not void but voidable. The property and right of possession in and to the chattel are divested, but, on repudiation of the contract, revert to the defrauded person, subject to any right acquired by third parties in the interval.

At the time the cheque was collected, in the absence of impersonation when it was obtained, it may well have been the property of the customer and therefore the banker may have no liability for conversion. If the customer had been named X, but in anticipation of stealing A's car, had opened the account in the name of A, then he may have impersonated A with the motor dealer. In that event, there would have been a conversion. Thus the bank having lost its statutory protection is liable if there has been a conversion. Whether this is so depends on whether the cheque belonged to the motor dealer when it was collected. It would have done if the transaction had been repudiated before the collection or if the cheque had been handed to the payee by the dealer in the belief that the payee was a different person. Otherwise there was probably no conversion and no liability on the part of the bank.

7 : Presumption of payment of cheque tendered for collection

The A Branch of the Southtown Bank Ltd collected on behalf of its important customers Z Co. Ltd a crossed cheque for £100 drawn on the B Branch of the Westown Bank Ltd. The cheque was despatched for collection through the general clearing in the usual way on Wednesday 29 April and nothing further was heard about the transaction until Tuesday 5 May, when an unpaid claim slip from the Westown Bank Ltd was received through the clearing.

On making enquiries from the Westown Bank Ltd it was found that the cheque had been returned unpaid marked Refer to Drawer *through the post, direct to the Southtown Bank Ltd on 1 May.*

The customers of the Southtown Bank Ltd refuse to allow their account to be debited with the amount of the cheque in view of the lapse of time and claim that as they had not been informed that the cheque had been returned unpaid by 4 May, they were entitled to assume that it was paid and had accordingly on that day, despatched goods to their customer.

Assuming the cheque does not come to hand, are the Southtown Bank Ltd in a position to debit their customer's account and what is the position of the Southtown Bank Ltd in relation to the Westown Bank Ltd?

It is recognised immediately that, at all events from a legal standpoint, this is a difficult question. In practice the good relationship between banker and customer may often enable a satisfactory solution to be achieved without reference to the legal elements involved.

There are really three questions : whether the customer has a claim; what the basis of the claim would be; and where the loss if any should fall. The first point to consider is the relevance of the Clearing House Rules. Although there may be differing views as to whether a customer can claim the benefit of such rules as well as be subjected to the burden by custom, or more precisely, by implication, there is no doubt that a banker may invoke those rules. That is to say that it is an implied term of the banker-customer contract that cheques shall be collected and paid in accordance with the Rules of the Clearing House and that, if the banker follows out those rules he is not liable for any consequence. The use of the Clearing House is necessary to the business efficacy of modern banking and may therefore be regarded as implied. By those rules a dishonoured cheque is returned direct, using the post. Although the Post Office is normally the agent of the sender, where there is an implied invitation from the other party to use the post then the collection is effected on behalf of the second party – that is the recipient for whose credit the cheque is paid in. Thus from the standpoint of the failure of the method of collection there can be no liability of the banker to the customer. He is tied to the Clearing House rules and if these have been followed the Southtown Bank has no liability to him for breach of contract – as would have been the case, for example, if that bank had mislaid the cheque on its own premises for a week. The further point may be taken as to whether, as a party to a dishonoured cheque, he is entitled to a notice of such dishonour. Here again the courts will uphold usage. By Section 49(15) of the Bills of Exchange Act where notice of dishonour is sent by post it is valid notwithstanding miscarriage by the post office. Incidentally, the use of the Clearing House was recognised in *Royal Bank of Ireland* v. *O'Rourke* (1962 I.R. 159). There appears to be only one possible basis upon which a customer may have a claim. If by a notice – printed on paying-in slips or intimated in some other way – the Southtown Bank has said that cheques may be 'regarded as paid' after a certain lapse of time or perhaps even merely indicating that they may not be drawn against until so many days after being tendered for collection, then such additional notice, dependent on its terms, may have amounted to a representation and thus have added to the rights that the customer might otherwise have.

Even in the event of there being a basis of claim, it would be very unlikely that the customer could refuse to be debited and regard the matter as at an end – presumably leaving the Southtown Bank to take what action it could as 'holder in due course' of the cheque. The customer may have drawn on the account in anticipation of payment of the cheque, but although such cheque should be paid the measure of his loss is not necessarily the amount of the cheque. He has merely had late advice. Of course if goods had been released to the payee then the customer would be able to claim whatever loss ensued; if, for example, action against the purchaser was worthless then the full amount of the cheque (less any dividend on his bankruptcy) could be claimed. All this is, as indicated, only in the event of there having been a firm representation by notice to customers entitling the customer to presume payment *as distinct from authorising him to* draw against the cheque. If the authority is to draw against the cheque, there is a breach only if the cheque so drawn is dishonoured.

If such a claim could be maintained there would be no responsibility on the Westown Bank, since it had merely followed the Clearing Rules. The loss, if any, would be that of the Southtown Bank.

8 : Cheque crossed *Account payee only*

John Brown, who is a customer of the Main Bank Ltd, but about whose background very little is known, one day pays in a batch of cheques for the credit of his account. Amongst these is one for £50, drawn by Jack Smith in favour of Bill Jones or order, bearing an endorsement 'Bill Jones' and, across its face, the words account payee only, *without the usual transverse parallel lines or any other words meant for a crossing. The cashier accepts the cheque, without any inquiry, and it is duly cleared. Some days later Bill Jones telephones the Main Bank, saying that, even though he had endorsed the £50 cheque, it had subsequently been stolen by Brown and paid into his account. Jones threatens to sue the Bank for negligence in collecting the cheque.*
What is the Bank's position?

In the 17th century the Common Law Courts recognised the principle that the custom prevailing between merchants could originate a legal duty. *Woodward* v. *Roe* 1666. The custom of marking cheques *Account payee* is at least as old as *Bellamy* v. *Marjoribanks* 1852. It is not a crossing, nor is it mentioned in the Bills of Exchange Act, 1882. Although it does not constitute an unlawful addition to an authorised crossing within Section 79 of the same Act, *Akrokerri (Atlantic) Mines Ltd.* v. *Economic Bank* 1904, it does not restrict the negotiability of the cheque. (*National Bank* v. *Silke* 1891). It has no statutory basis but it has been recognised by case law, and its effect is merely to put the banker on inquiry; and he ignores it at his peril. If the banker finds his inquiries are reasonably answered, he may still lose the protection of Sec. 4, Cheques Act 1957, amending Sec. 82, Bills of Exchange Act 1882. The crux of the section is 'negligence'; it is the banker's action or lack of it which makes him vulnerable to a case of conversion of a cheque. In *Bevan* v. *National Bank Ltd.* 1906, where the bank did make enquiries and received satisfactory replies, the judge emphasised that to disregard words of this kind would amount to negligence, and that a bank is put on inquiry if a cheque so marked is to be credited otherwise than to the payee's account.

The collection of such a cheque for a person other than the payee is only *prima facia* evidence of negligence, as it does not conclusively prove negligence. *Morison* v. *London, County & Westminster Bank* 1914. The later case of *House Property Co. of London* v. *London, County & Westminster Bank* 1915 confirmed that it is negligence to collect such a cheque payable to a named payee or bearer for an account other than that of the named payee. This further limits the negotiability of the cheque which basically the Bills of Exchange Act makes negotiable.

It is curious that the drawer of a cheque can give an effective instruction to a banker with whom he may not have any contractual relationship. The banker has to protect the rights of the true owner, with whom he has no dealings; and the only recognisable duty is the unilateral statutory one on the collecting banker not to be negligent. Lord Atkin in *Midland Bank Ltd.* v. *Reckett & Ors.* 1933 stated that under Sec. 82, good faith was not challenged, but the onus of proving the absence of negligence was plainly cast upon the bank. But for the section they are liable for conversion, and it is for them to bring themselves within the statutory protection. It is important to note here that the cheques concerned were used to liquidate an overdraft; and it was at the bank's repeated requests to reduce the debt that cheques were misapplied to the account. Also, Lord Atkin in this case re-iterated his own words used in *Underwood's Case* 1924 : 'the bank so disposed of the chattels, the cheques, as to deprive both themselves and the true owners of the dominion over them, and in exchange for the pieces of paper constituted themselves the debtors of the customer. I cannot imagine a plainer case of conversion'.

As the welter of cases increases, stressing the bank's bounden duty to inquire, we must consider the practical facts of the problem. John Brown is a customer, about whom little is known, and the cheque in question was paid in amongst others without any inquiry. A similar case arose in *Ladbroke* v. *Todd* 1914 and it has accordingly become necessary for a banker to inquire more carefully, and to satisfy himself on reasonable grounds that cheques are indeed the property of his customer. This was confirmed in *Lloyds Bank Ltd.* v. *Savory* 1933. It is well established that a banker should make full inquiries and take references when opening an account. Such references must be satisfactory and checked upon as to their veracity, before the account is conducted, particularly if cheques are tendered and a check book is requested. It is not incumbent upon the banker to be constantly watching his customer's activities nor is it possible in large city offices, so that the

58

bank not having much knowledge of Mr John Brown's background is not entirely negligence, provided they opened the account correctly and checked upon his references.

It may be argued that when the cashier took the cheque it was an oversight; perhaps he was busy, short staffed or just did not notice the words. Judicial opinions vary in this point. Bailache J. in *Ross* v. *London, County, Westminster and Parr's Bank* 1919 considered that the same standard of care and experience was not expected from a cashier as from a bank manager, and Sankey L.J., in *Lloyds Bank* v. *Chartered Bank of India, Australia and China* 1928 said that it is not expected that officials of banks should also be amateur detectives; and his co-judge opined that a thorough history of each cheque would render business impracticable. Conversely, in *Crumplin* v. *London Joint Stock Bank* 1913 Pickford J., stated it was no defence for a bank to say they were too busy or had insufficient staff to make inquiries. He added that if the bank could not make inquiries when necessary they must take the consequences.

While the case against Main Bank Ltd. may seem to be heavily weighted, there may be some circumstances condoning negligence and it is advisable to consider these factors. What might appear as negligence may be condoned if the acts or omissions as evidence of negligence were induced or encouraged by the action or inaction of the true owner. In 1940, the defence of contributory negligence was established by the House of Lords and a few years later the Law Reform (Contributory Negligence) Act 1945 was passed. From the Main Bank's position, a number of queries may now be considered. The problem states some days later 'the payee, Bill Jones, presumably unknown to the bank, notified them of the theft. First, can the bank accept a third person's statement as true without corroboration. Secondly, if Mr Jones knew that Mr Brown (not just some person or other) had stolen the cheque why did not Mr Jones instruct the drawer to stop the cheque immediately, and not take action some days later. One may ask 'is there contributory negligence'? Mr Jones is making a very serious statement of theft, to a bank about its customer, Mr Brown and is open to an action for slander. Again, if Mr Jones is so confident of a case against Mr Brown, why then did he not take action immediately against Mr Brown, instead of going behind his back and threatening the bank?

Mr Brown is the customer of Main Bank Ltd, and, at present, it is to him their duty lies. Looked at from this angle, it seems remarkable that

Brown paying in a batch of cheques and therefore having knowledge of banking procedure would pay in a stolen cheque marked *account payee only,* knowing full well that the cheque could very easily be traced back to him. So the question arises as to whether other cheques – third party or account payee – are commonly paid in by Mr Brown. It may be that previous cheques, similarly marked, payable to the same payee and issued by the same drawer have been queried by the Main Bank on prior occasions, and explanations provided by Mr Brown may have been satisfactory. In which case another cheque having been paid in, the bank may have assumed it too was in order.

It has been suggested that *account payee only* has a different significance from *account payee.* Atkin, L.J. in *Allied Importers* v. *Westminster Bank Ltd.* 1927 stated it would be difficult to differentiate. On the other hand it contended that the words *account payee only* in the handwriting of the drawer has the same effect as making the cheque 'Pay AB only' and the practice is thus discouraged by the London Clearing Bankers. There is also the possibility that Mr Brown's account was overdrawn and had he been pressed for repayment.

The recent case of *Marfani* v. *Midland Bank Ltd.* 1967 is worthy of study although not concerning *account payee*; it does confirm the points regarding opening accounts and negligence as enumerated above. It is the practice of bankesr to accept cheques marked *account payee* for other than the payee's account providing their customer is of undoubted integrity and preferably of long standing and also provided the cheque is for a small amount relatively.

There are equal grounds that Bill Jones's story is not true. If John Brown has not stolen it, but has given value for it, then he is a holder in due course and could rightly claim the money from the drawer even if payment had been stopped : Sec. 29, Bills of Exchange Act 1881. It often happens that a cheque marked *account payee only* is issued as a safeguard when sent through the post to a person who has no bank account. A banker may credit such a cheque to his customer's account, as in this case; but if the bank becomes liable for conversion it has a right to be indemnified by the customer, Mr Brown, in respect of the £50 claimed : *Adamson* v. *Jarvis* 1827. On the other hand, if the manager of a local shop misapplies cheques of his employer, the bank may lose its indemnity : *Baker* v. *Barclays Bank* 1955.

On the face of the facts given, the case against the Main Bank may seem very heavy. However, the bank may be able to substantiate further information to the effect that they had an implied authority from Bill Jones. Pending the inquiries Main Bank Ltd. would be well advised to keep a careful check upon the credits and debits of Mr Brown's account until the matter is settled.

NB : An alternative view is, however, that there are no circumstances in which a bank collecting a cheque crossed *account payee* or *account payee only* for the credit of an account other than that of the named payee can escape a successful action for conversion by the true owner of the cheque, who loses as a result of it being collected by the bank for the third party account. In other words, to collect such a cheque for a third party account is negligence that cannot be refuted unless the true owner (Bill Jones) is estopped by his own conduct in encouraging payment.

Part three : Bills and negotiation of cheques

Perhaps the most misunderstood aspect of bills of exchange is caused by the different meanings placed on the word 'negotiable'. In common parlance it means something that is saleable. In relation to cheques it means what may perhaps be described as 'full negotiability' in that a cheque crossed '*Not Negotiable*' is one that is fully transferable. However a transferor cannot give a transferee a better title than he, the transferor, had himself. In relation to a bill, however, the word 'negotiable' means transferability. In Section 8 (1) of the Bills of Exchange Act it is indicated that when the bill contains words prohibiting transfer it is merely valid between the parties 'but is not negotiable'. 'Not negotiable' in this context means not transferable. Of course, the ability of a transferee of a bill or of a fully negotiable cheque to enforce it for his own right is dependent upon his being a 'holder in due course' within the meaning of Section 29 of the Bills of Exchange Act, which necessitates: good faith, value, the bill not being 'overdue', its being complete and regular on the face of it, there being no notice of its previous dishonour or of defects in title of the previous holder.

As to the specific questions:

Question 1
The re-acceptance of a bill is frequently attempted. It is not effective here other than as a contract between particular parties or, possibly as a new bill, if all parties formally concur.

Question 2
This problem illustrates very well the effect of forgery in destroying the quality of negotiability.

Question 3
'Holder for value' is one of the most difficult things to understand. Briefly it falls short of 'Holder in due course' in that the holder himself need not have given value. The question, however, is indicative of the position of the banker as the 'Holder in due course' in that value has been given by the banker.

Question 4

The question relating to the holder of a stopped cheque reminds one that, although the subject has been litigated less than one would have expected, a cheque is a fully negotiable instrument. However, its enforceability is dependent upon value having been given by the holder.

/

1 : Attempted re-acceptance of a bill

ABC Bank Limited received shipping documents from their principals in a foreign country who instructed them to release the documents against acceptance of a 60-day bill. The bill of exchange was in due course accepted and the documents were released.

Before the acceptance is due instructions from the principals were received saying: 'Please extend the bills for a further 30 days from the original due dates and advise us, when re-accepted, of the new maturity dates'.

Discuss the action ABC Bank should take and in particular the legalities of 're-acceptance'.

The first point to observe is that where a document of title, such as a bill of lading, is tendered accompanied by a bill of exchange, that bill being presented for payment or acceptance, the property in the documents passes only upon payment or acceptance of the bill of exchange. This was established in the case of *Shepherd* v. *Harrison* (1871 L.R. 5 H.L. 116). The principle was further acknowledged in the case of *Cahn* v. *Pockett's Bristol Channel Co.* (1889 1 Q.B. 643), although in that instance a right to the bill was obtained by a third party to whom it was wrongfully negotiated by the party to whom a bill of exchange had been tendered for acceptance but by whom no acceptance had been given. This, however, is an illustration that in commercial transactions there is usually protection against the consequences of insolvency but not of fraud.

The next aspect – admittedly of more difficulty – concerns the extension of the bill. This is not known in English law, although it is a feature of some foreign legal systems. A bill may be subject to a qualified acceptance, although third parties are not bound, except in a case of a partial acceptance. There is however no provision for re-acceptance. It differs from acceptance for honour which follows the actual dishonour and is by a third party. If in fact a bill is extended the effect is an agreement between the holder and the acceptor. Those parties will be bound by what is a contract. The new obligation is not a bill of exchange and cannot bind other parties.

64

It must always be remembered that some of the parties may, however, be quite happy for this so-called extension to be effected because of the validity of such arrangements in other countries whose law may be applicable or where, possibly, litigation may take place, and such an extension may be a common-place occurrence. Reverting to the position obtaining in this country, it is of interest to see the reference in the *Journal* of the Institute of Bankers, January 1925, in which it was observed that re-accepted bills were really new bills. The note referred to a decision of the Bombay High Court reported in *The Times* of 29 November, 1924, in which it had been held that such a bill could not be admitted as evidence because the re-acceptance had not been stamped. (Probably it could have been stamped as a contract under penalty, but that aspect is not mentioned.) It adds that new bills should be issued, or the bills presented, dishonoured, noted, and then held until the new date for payment.

Turning to the specific question, the duty of the ABC Bank Ltd is to take instructions from the principals letting them know what appears to be the legal position here. If communication is not possible because of shortage of time it is desirable to present the bill, if by not doing so any party who would otherwise be liable escapes. If *all* parties consent, then, in the absence of instructions, re-acceptance can be effected. It is necessary to add a new stamp. This is now only two pence so some of the difficulty previously surrounding the problem is diminished.

E

2 : Liability on a transferred cheque

Jones, a wholesaler, supplies goods to Davis, a retailer, who pays Jones by cheque. Jones passes the cheque to E for goods supplied, but E loses the cheque. F finds the cheque, forges endorsement and obtains goods from G, to whom he passes the cheque. G in turn purchases goods from H and passes the cheque on to him. Finally, H presents the instrument to his bank, whereupon it is returned 'payment stopped'. G and H were unaware of the forgery. Thus E and H are unpaid, but Davis the drawer has not paid for his goods. ·

What is the position of the parties concerned, and would it have made any difference if E had endorsed the cheque before he lost it?

It is to be recognised that the sequence described will not happen very often because a cheque does not pass from hand to hand (unlike the silver dollar!) so frequently. The holder will generally pay it into his account. On the other hand such sequence may occur in practice, especially where the parties do not wish to draw their own cheques. Associated with the transfer is the question of the cheque being stale for the purpose of negotiation. A cheque, being a bill of exchange payable on demand, is overdue when it has been in circulation for an unreasonable length of time (Bills of Exchange Act, 1882, Section 36(3)); what is a reasonable length of time is a question of fact; a cheque negotiated eight days after date has been held not to be overdue whereas one negotiated two months after date has been held to be overdue (that is 'overdue' in this sense as distinct from the cheque that the paying banker calls 'stale' because it is more than six months after date and he requires his customer's confirmation before he will pay it). There is of course the question of whether the length of time a cheque has been in circulation is affected by the number of occasions during the period that it has been transferred; a cheque transferred four times within three weeks might be regarded differently from one which has been in circulation for the same length of time but which has been transferred only once within the period. The same length of time may be unreasonable in one case and not in the other. For the purpose of the question it is being assumed that the transfers were

66

effected within a reasonable length of time after the original date of issue.

The first point to notice is that where the endorsement of E is forged no subsequent holder can claim through that forged signature. Therefore neither G nor H can sue Davis or Jones or E. This position is clear from section 24 of the Bills of Exchange Act, which states that no right to enforce payment can be acquired through such a signature. There are a number of exceptions but that is the general principle. One right preserved is that an earlier holder cannot deny to a subsequent holder the genuineness of the signature of the prior endorser or of the drawer, Thus G cannot claim as against H that, because this cheque contains a forgery and is a void instrument, he does not have to reimburse H. Section 55 (2)(c) of the Act states this specifically.

Now let us look at the position of the parties. H can claim against G who must reimburse him for the amount of the cheque. If G can find F he can of course claim from him; in all probability, even then F may be impecunious. G cannot claim from E or from Jones or Davis, the drawer, because the signature of E is forged and no claim can be made through a forged signature against prior holders. E who has lost the cheque is entitled, as its true owner, to claim it from G (who has had to reimburse H). E can then claim from the drawer who will thus pay for the goods he has received. If the whereabouts of the cheque had not been discovered E could have demanded a duplicate from Davis against an indemnity suitably secured (Bills of Exchange Act, section 69). If that had been done E would have been at no risk (apart perhaps from unrecovered costs of any proceedings) because Davis, the drawer, could have refuted G's claim as mentioned above.

Had E endorsed the cheque before losing it, the position would have been quite different. There would have been no forgery and if the cheque had been fully negotiable F (the finder who has a bad title) would have been able to give G a better title than he himself had. That is to say, H would have been a holder in due course (Section 29) and could have sued any of the earlier parties, as could G have done, for example, if H had chosen to sue G. However in such circumstances if the cheque had been crossed *not negotiable* the position would have been different. By Section 81 of the Bills of Exchange Act, G would have had no better title than F. F's title was bad and therefore G, although liable to H, could not sue E or Jones or Davis. G would be the loser since he must pay H for the goods received and cannot sue any of the previous holders of the cheque, although he can, of course, sue F.

3 : The banker as a holder for value

Mr X is being pressed by his bankers to reduce his overdraft. His monthly salary is by cheque made payable to his bankers *for the credit of his account. Following a previous warning letter to Mr X, the bank, upon receipt of a subsequent salary cheque for £100, credit his account and write to inform his that they are not prepared to allow any withdrawals against this cheque, the proceeds of which must be applied in reduction of his borrowing.*

Two days later Mr X informs the bank that he has filed his petition in bankruptcy. The following day the cheque is returned marked 'Orders not to pay' and the bank receives the usual notification from the Official Receiver that a receiving order was made the previous day.

1. Can the bank debit Mr X's account with the £100 and include it in their proof of claim?

2. Has the bank any legal remedy against the drawer of the cheque and if so what action should they take?

3. Would the position be any different if the bank had not been pressing for reductions?

The first of the three questions is relatively simple. When a banker collects a cheque for a customer he is that customer's agent. Automatically he has a right to reimbursement if that cheque is returned; that is to say, he *may* debit his customer's account. The fact that there has been notice of an act of bankruptcy, or of a petition, or that there has been a receiving order made, after the cheque has been credited to the account but before it is returned, does not affect the right of the banker to re-debit the amount of the returned cheque. His right flows from the terms under which he received the cheque for collection and the trustee cannot claim any better right in that connection than could the bankrupt himself. Even in the case where a banker negotiates a draft or becomes a 'holder in due course' or a 'holder for value' the right to re-debit the amount to the account exists. Accordingly the banker, as one may expect, can prove. Whether it is desirable or wise to re-debit the account where the banker is claiming

68

on the drawer is a point to which reference is made below. However, if he does not recover fully from other sources he may prove for the debit balance in his books.

The second question is one of difficulty. The circumstances are such that the banker may be regarded as being in an equivalent position to receiving the cheque in specific reduction of the overdraft. He has intimated that he will pay no further cheques and demanded reductions. *In practice* it is of course true that a banker would adopt such a rigorous line of action only with the most unscrupulous of customers, although the position may be affected if it is thought that bankruptcy is imminent. Feasibly, the cheque was received because the customer had failed in an attempt to obtain his salary in cash. Whatever may be the practical background, the circumstances are such that the banker would probably be able to establish that he was a holder in due course – *if this had been necessary or of advantage to him.* In this case he is the *payee,* albeit for the account of his customer. As a payee there is no question of his having the rights of a holder in due course (*R. E. Jones* v. *Waring & Gillow* 1926 A.C. 670). His right to the benefit of the cheque *vis-à-vis* the drawer's, that is the customer's employers, is as good as that of the employee. Thus if the employee had a right to the wages, the banker, it is submitted, could sue the employer. The notice of the bankruptcy events would not enable the drawers to refuse payment to the payee. The better view is also that the trustee in bankruptcy could not claim the benefit of the cheque from the bank because of the manner in which it was drawn. In the case of *Re Keever* (1967 Ch. 182) it was held that a collecting banker had a lien on a cheque payable to a customer despite the proceeds having been received after the date of the Receiving Order.

Where a cheque received for collection is dishonoured and a banker wishes to claim against the drawer it has been held that if he returns the cheque to the customer unconditionally he cannot sue (*Lloyds Bank* v. *Dolphin* 1920 : see *Legal Decisions Affecting Bankers* Vol. III, page 230), although the decision was criticised by Sir Mackenzie Chalmers. The risk is emphasised by the decision of *Westminster Bank* v. *Zang* (1966 1 AER 114). It is thus desirable to debit a suspense account to avoid the suggestion that the banker has foregone his rights.

The third question relates to pressure. Without this, of course, the banker may not have received the payment at all. Pressure, however, would obviate any suggestion of there having been a fraudulent preference since it would exclude any contention that there had been a dominant intention on the part of the bankrupt to prefer the bank. It also establishes that the payment to the banker is not merely (with the intention of the banker) receiving the money as an agent but as a creditor.

4 : The rights of a holder of a stopped cheque

Mrs A, a customer of Northtown Bank, instructed B, a small builder, to carry out some repairs to a chimney stack. He asked for an advance of cash and was given a cheque for £20. He did not arrive to do the work two days later as promised and Mrs A discovered that he was not at the address that he had given her. Thereupon she gave orders to the Northtown Bank to stop the cheque. These instructions were obeyed and it transpired that B had encashed the cheque with a publican, P, to whom he was unknown.

What are the rights of P, the publican, against Mrs A?
What would have been the position of the bank had they failed to obey the order to countermand payment?

There is one simple and one difficult aspect to this question. The former concerns a principle well known to bankers. It reminds one that a cheque is a form of a bill of exchange and therefore, in the absence of a 'non negotiable' crossing, a transferee can get a better title than the transferor. As a holder in due course can sue the drawer in the event of non-payment, the first part of the answer depends on two questions if it is shown that Mrs A was justified in stopping the cheque: was the cheque crossed *not negotiable*? and if not was P a holder in due course? If the cheque bore a 'not negotiable' crossing then, although P took the cheque complete and regular on its face for value, in good faith, without notice in the defect of the title of B and without notice of previous dishonour, thus being a 'holder in due course', he could not get a better title than B. He could therefore sue Mrs A only if he could establish that B's claim against Mrs A was good. If, however, the cheque bore no 'not negotiable' crossing, P could sue Mrs A irrespective of whether she, as between herself and the builder B, was justified in countermanding payment. Two cases where bankers themselves have paid against cheques before clearance and become holders in due course, as did the publican in the present instance, illustrate the principle; namely *Midland Bank* v. *Charles Simpson Motors Ltd.* (1960 Legal Decisions Affecting Bankers Vol. 7, p. 25) and *Barclays Bank* v. *Harding* (Journal of the Institute of Bankers

Vol. 83, p. 109). Of course, if Mrs A was not justified in stopping the cheque in favour of B then, even if there was a 'not negotiable' crossing, P has given value to B and has the same rights as B.

The more difficult aspect is whether Mrs A was entitled to stop the cheque. The first point to realise is that when a cheque has been given, the onus of proof that the holder has no title lies upon the person being sued. If, for example, no cheque had been given, and Mrs A had not paid B, B would have had the task of proving that the order had been given and carried out (unless by arrangement he was entitled to payment before the work was done). As, however, a cheque had been given, indicating *prima facie* that B was entitled to receive money, the onus of establishing the contrary lay upon Mrs A. This would be so if the cheque was crossed 'not negotiable' and P was suing her with the same rights only as B. The most difficult question is whether Mrs A would succeed in establishing that she was not liable on the cheque. To do this she would have to establish that it was obtained by fraud and that therefore the consideration was bad or that there was no consideration. The latter question does not arise since there was a promise to do work and one promise given in exchange for another is a good consideration. The remaining point, therefore, is whether fraud could be established on the part of the builder B. The mere fact that he did not attend on the date promised is a breach of contract but not fraud. If, of course, the building business eventuates to be non-existent then there would be blatant fraud and only a holder in due course could sue Mrs A. The giving of the wrong address could have been accidental, but otherwise it would be part of the evidence of fraud. If there was a genuine business in the name of B, it is unlikely that the wrong address would be enough to set up fraud.

If the bank had paid the stopped cheque, Mrs A's account would have had to be re-credited, but, if the work had been carried out by the builder B, then Mrs A would subsequently have had to repay the £20 to the bank. If the builder had been fraudulent and Mrs A had not been liable because of a 'not negotiable' crossing, then the bank loses the money apart from its rights against B, which may be worthless. If Mrs A was liable on the cheque, then she has lost nothing and the bank is entitled to recover the money which it must immediately re-credit to her account while the position is under investigation.

To summarise :

1. P can sue Mrs A if there is no *not negotiable* crossing and he is 'holder in due course'.

2. If there is a 'not negotiable' crossing or P is not a holder in due course, he has no better rights than B, the builder.

3. If B was fraudulent then he has no rights – this may be difficult to prove.

4. The bank, if it pays the stopped cheque, has rights against Mrs A only if she herself could have been sued on the cheque she stopped or she enjoys a benefit from the payment of the cheque.

Part four : Guarantees

The first thing to appreciate relating to a guarantee is that it is an accessory contract. If the principle debtor is liable the guarantor is liable. On the other hand, an indemnity – like an insurance policy – although sometimes achieving the same thing, is an undertaking to be responsible for the ultimate loss. This can sometimes have different consequences, especially if the principal debt is technically unenforceable when usually a guarantor is released. The other dominant factor is that bank guarantee forms take away from the guarantor many of the rights that he would otherwise have and give the bank extra rights, such as to hold assets of the guarantor as security for the guarantee. More caution is necessary than at the date of the First Edition in relation to undue influence on a guarantor, especially when the guarantor is another customer of the bank to whom a possible duty may be owed.

As to the questions:

Question 1
This illustrates the accessory nature of the guarantee.

Question 2
This reflects the specific clause contained in a guarantee in favour of the bank. The decision in *Garnett* v. *McKewan* has now been approved by the House of Lords in *Halesowen Pressworks and Assemblies Ltd.* v. *Westminster Bank Ltd.* (1972 A.C. 875)

Question 3
This question relating to the duration of a guarantee deals with a subject of maximum importance in practice in that guarantees are to secure current accounts.

Question 4
There are difficult undecided legal aspects here; the practical course is obviously to provide for the contingency in the form of guarantee.

74

1 : Guarantors and a preferential debt

Anytown Bank's customer, A.B. Limited has an overdraft secured by the joint and several guarantees of the directors for £10,000. The directors are known to be entirely good for this liability. The company, somewhat under-capitalised, has been in excess of the limit on numerous occasions in the past and the bank has called some months ago for a wages account to be opened. This account has been correctly operated by the bank and repayments made from the company's current account as and when necessary.

The company has now gone into liquidation following the non-payment of certain accounts and at the date of the winding-up order the bank accounts stood as follows:

Current account	Dr.	£1,490
Wages account	Dr.	£8,570

The company's balance sheet comprised the following:

Capital	200	Goodwill	3,000
Creditors	10,740	Premises (Leasehold)	2,000
Bank	10,060	Debtors	6,800
		Directors Loans	2,500
		Profit and loss account	6,700
	£21,000		£21,000

Of the other creditors £1,240 were also preferential.

As regards obtaining repayment of its advances, what courses are open to the bank and which of these should be adopted?

The following assessment of the situation set out in this problem disregards liquidation expenses and accrued bank charges, and it assumes that the loans to the directors are not in contravention of S.190 of the Companies Act 1948.* It has also been assumed that the directors' guarantee has been taken on a document drawn in the customary bank form which would have the effect of preventing the guarantors from proving in the liquidation in competition with the bank until such time as the whole debt to the bank, and not merely that part for which they are liable, had been cleared.

Before turning to the courses which the liquidation might take, it will be helpful to look at the balance sheet figures. On the liabilities side, the shareholders can, of course, look only to any surplus which might remain after all the other claims have been met in full; the £200 capital item must therefore be ignored until that time. On the assets side, profit and loss – on the wrong side of the balance sheet – represents accumulated losses and is of no practical value. Similarly, goodwill must be disregarded since it exists only in a going concern, and there are thus only three realisable assets: premises £2,000, debtors £6,800 and directors' loans £2,500; and it will be assumed in the following calculations that each realises the balance sheet figures.

The Bankruptcy Act 1914 details the alternatives open to a creditor holding security which is the property of the debtor, but provides that third party security may be treated as collateral security. The effect of this is that it may be disregarded in submitting the proof of debt, but is available to meet any deficit when the final dividend has been paid. S.317 of the Companies Act 1948 extends these provisions to the liquidation of a company registered in England.

There are thus two alternative courses of action within the initiative of the bank, who may *either* call on the guarantors, place the amount received in repayment of the current account and reduction of the wages account and prove as preferential creditors for the remaining £60, *or* prove for the whole debt to the bank, calling on the guarantors only for the remaining deficit. In any event it must be remembered that the guarantors can make no claim against the company's assets until the bank has been repaid *in full*.

Examining the first alternative, the realisable assets total £11,300, while the first claims of preferential creditors total £1,300 (*i.e.*, the bank's remaining £60 and the others, stated to be £1,240). There is thus a fund of £10,000 from which to meet the claims of the unsecured creditors (£9,500) and, when the bank has received dividends totalling £60, of the guarantors. The Directors therefore have to find £12,500 (£10,000 to meet their guarantee liability and £2,500 to repay their loans) less whatever they are able to recover when they are able to submit a proof (and they cannot claim to have the distribution of any previous dividend disturbed). They can prove as soon as the bank is repaid.

While it is possible that the effect on the directors' pockets may be no more than just, there is a not unnatural reluctance on the part of creditors to call on sureties to a greater extent than is necessary. Partly for this reason, but mainly because it enables the bank to gather in the greatest possible sum in those cases where a loss is anticipated, the second alternative is adopted. The liquidation accounts in this case appear as follows:

Realisable assets   £11,300
less Preferential creditors –
    Bank   £8,570
    Others £1,240 – £9,810 *met in full*
        leaving £1,490

to pay a dividend of 2s. 8d. in the pound on the £10,990 owing to the unsecured creditors, including the bank's claim on the current account. The bank's dividend on this debt is approximately £198, leaving the guarantors to provide the remaining £1,292 in addition to having repaid their loans. Any payment volunteered by the guarantors before distribution of the final liquidation dividend would be placed to a suspense account by the bank, as provided for by the terms of its guarantee, and not applied directly to the overdrawn accounts.

However, there is a third alternative, the initiative for which lies not with the bank but with the guarantors, and in the circumstances of this particular case it is this one which is most likely to be adopted. If the guarantors pay to the bank not only their guarantee liability but the whole debt to the bank, there is no longer any bar to their proving in the liquidation from the outset. Moreover, since S.319 of the Companies Act, which leads to the use of separate wages accounts, does not restrict its benefit to bankers, they can prove as preferential creditors for the amount of the wages account balance. Further, by S.31 of the Bankruptcy Act, which again applies also to company liquidations in

*Since the question was submitted the exempt private company has been abolished by the Companies Act 1967 but that aspect is not relevant to the main points of the answer

England, the directors' loans must be set off before proof is submitted, so that the computation would appear thus :

	Preferential	Unsecured	Total
Debts to guarantors	£8,570	£1,490	£10,060
Loans set off	—£1,010	—£1490	£2,500
Guarantors prove for	£7,560	Nil	

Remaining Realisable Assets £8,800 (that is *less* Directors' Loan) *less* Preferential Creditors—

G'tors £7,560
Others £1,240 – £8,800   *met in full*

By this means the bank is satisfied, and the directors discharge their legal obligations at a cost of only £2,560 – a cost considerably less than in the other alternatives which have been considered. Admittedly, this is achieved to the detriment of the unsecured creditors, but the moralities of laws which can allow directors to reduce their personal loss, in a situation which might be the result of their own mis-management, at the expense of innocent third parties, do not fall to be considered here.

It is to be noted that in practice the claim would have been reduced in all probability to the extent that the money withdrawn for wages was outside the preferential limits or was used for other purposes.

2 : Set-off against a guarantor

Your customer A is overdrawn £500. The account is secured by the guarantee of B, also a customer, for £500. Having failed to obtain repayment from A, you make demand on B, whose account is £750 in credit. Fearing that B may attempt to avoid his liability, you transfer £500 from his account in reduction of the debt. The following day cheques for £450 are presented on B's account. You return them 'Refer to Drawer'. Are your actions justified?

There are three aspects that are likely to dominate the practical decision taken by a banker faced with the problem described. First, the giving of notice is likely to have the effect of the money being withdrawn, since the guarantor who leaves his money on the account will pay readily and/or has available assets. Secondly, the wording on the form of guarantee may refer specifically to the balance on the account of the guarantor, in which event the answer will depend on what is stated in the guarantee. Thirdly, the banker will be conscious, very rightly, of the measure of damage resulting from the dishonour which may be much more than the aggregate amount of the cheques dishonoured.

It is perhaps reasonable first to indicate the position relating to set-off generally in relation to bank accounts. The better view is that the decision of the Court of Appeal in *Garnet* v. *McKewan* (1872) L.R. 8 Ex. 10 is correct in that the banker has a right of set-off in the absence of an indication of a contrary agreement. The case usually advanced to the contrary (*Greenhalgh* v. *Union Bank of Manchester* (1924) 2 K.B. 153) may be regarded as subject to its particular facts. The existence of two accounts *may* reflect a decision to keep them separate or be evidence supporting such a contention, but such agreement cannot be inferred automatically from the existence of the two accounts. That is to say, the right to combine without a period of notice is not excluded if there are a number of different accounts. When a demand is made on the guarantor, B, then a debt becomes due from him – not by reason of the conduct of a banking account – but because he gave a guarantee.

Now if that guarantee provides specifically for that event, then the question is beyond all doubt. Two parties can contract for what results they like in all but very few instances. From the banker's standpoint it is better to state specifically what is to happen. A form of guarantee may provide for a 'lien' on the guarantor's assets. Although the right to hold money against a money liability is strictly a set-off, the term 'lien' is often used to include money as well as other assets such as securities, to which it is more appropriate. It is also relevant to quote *Questions on Banking Practice* No. 775 (1952 Edn.) which in the following terms expresses the view that a right of set-off arises as soon as demand is made.

Question. Can the credit balance of a guarantor's account be held as a set-off against his liability under the guarantee?

Answer. If the guarantee is payable on demand, no debt is owing by the guarantor to the bank until demand is made (*Bradford Old Bank* v. *Sutcliffe,* 1918, 2 K.B. 833) and accordingly until then there can be no right of set-off. As soon as demand has been made the right of set-off is exercisable. Some guarantees however specifically provide a right of set-off without demand (strictly this is in law probably a charge).

Even without any provision in the guarantee the common law position of a debtor and creditor is such that the creditor may when bringing an action combine to sue for a net balance. Similarly the position when proving in an insolvency necessitates the net amount being claimed. This admittedly does not mean necessarily that the banker-customer relationship of itself lays open a credit balance, which of its nature is intended for the drawing of cheques, to any cash claims the banker may have. Yet the decision of *Garnet* v. *McKewan* relates to a current account and therefore appears to justify such a view, despite the contractual banker-customer relationship affecting the credit balance.

In practice the dishonouring of cheques is looked at askance. Of course if the customer has a bad record then it is felt that his credit cannot be much worsened. When a customer is 'undoubted', on the other hand, a banker would not think of setting off a balance, because recovery is available in other ways. The circumstances thus often make for a solution in practice with less difficulty than in theory. It may sometimes be that the banker informs the customer that the credit balance should not be used but pays outstanding cheques.

To summarise it is suggested –

(1) If the guarantee alludes to the position, directly or indirectly, its terms govern the position.

80

(2) If the guarantee is silent on the point the balance demanded still becomes due and can be set-off in the absence of contrary agreement.

(3) The banker should be hesitant to dishonour cheques genuinely dated prior to the demand.

(4) In any event dishonour of cheques is to be avoided if possible.

(5) When there is insolvency and the bank is proving there is no question of doing other than setting off the amounts.

F

3 : The duration of a guarantee

Three years ago Northtown Bank deemed it necessary to call in an unsatisfactory advance made to a professional customer, Mr A. The position was then as follows:

Balance Dr. £5,500 – security, guarantee by Mr G, £2,000, and Life Policy (direct security) £5,000 (surrender value £2,600).

On default by the customer, the account was broken, demand was made upon Mr G, and a new account opened for future operations by Mr A, to be maintained in credit. Mr G settled his liability in cash, and £2,000 was credited to a guarantee security account, the guarantee being retained uncancelled.

The next twelve months or so saw Mr A established as a prominent public figure, and, after a time, temporary overdrafts, of a few days duration, were occasionally allowed by the bank on the new account, against outstanding professional fees.

A letter from the bank requesting an immediate remittance to cover the current overdraft of £450, which had persisted for two weeks, brought the following reply from Mr A:

'My life policy (your security), which matures next month, will produce sufficient to repay the net sum due in respect of my original debt, namely £3,500, together with the new account debt of £450, plus your charges; the residual balance, to the £100, please invest in Defence Bonds on my behalf. Incidentally, I have now repaid my liability to Mr G, in respect of his Guarantee.

Yours faithfully,

Mr A.'

Can Northtown Bank appropriate the policy proceeds in the manner suggested? If not, how should proceeds be allocated? Would the position be different if no mention had been made in the letter of the payment to Mr G?

In considering the problem the banker can look first at the legal position and then decide the practical course he is going to adopt.

There is the common law position to note. When a guarantor pays off a debt he has a right to any security held from the principal debtor. Even if he pays off only part he may claim to have any surplus proceeds of security. As with other common law rights, of which a guarantor is deprived by signing the bank form, the object of a banker in taking these rights is to cover errors and contingencies. The policy of a banker, as is discussed below, is generally speaking to deal with the parties in such a way as he would be bound to do in the absence of protective provisions under the guarantee. Turning to the immediate problem it will be found that in most, if not all, bank forms of guarantee there is a clause enabling a bank to place monies received from a guarantor on a suspense account. There is also power given to open a new account and the guarantor gives up his right to claim any security. The latter provision would not operate if the banker had been repaid in full but still has effect when there is indebtedness or obligation outstanding, despite the fact that the guarantor may have paid up the maximum amount due from him.

There is one more legal aspect to be examined. Once a demand is made on the guarantor he well may have no further liability for future advances. This may depend on the wording of the particular guarantee. Usually there is an undertaking to meet all the principal debtor's liabilities until the guarantee is determined by notice or demand. Such clauses are construed strictly by the courts against the banker because it is his document; therefore, the more explicit the form in this connection the more satisfactory is the transaction. Thus whilst the banker is protected against most of the contingencies he will not normally recover in respect of an account continued after the date of demand. However, as mentioned this may depend upon the wording of its particular clauses. In the case of *Westminster Bank* v. *Cond* (1940) 40 Com. Cas 60 there is an example of a clause that enabled the bank to sue notwithstanding the failure to break an account.

It now remains to decide what the bank should do and by what method. The general policy is to be as fair as possible to all concerned. The above-mentioned legal provisions place bankers in a strong position and protect them if it proves difficult for practical purposes to treat all parties equitably. Communication with customers may not be possible or the conduct of some of the parties concerned may appear to have offended decent commercial principles; or the banker may make a mistake. In all these instances the legal clauses of the guarantee come to his aid. Yet they are the very rare exceptions in practice.

In the question, the branch manager will wish, from a policy stand-point at all events, to be satisfied that the guarantor has been reim-bursed by A. (In fact, in relation to the £450 he will need to do so from a legal standpoint). This information he can ascertain informally from the guarantor Mr G. He can telephone him and make, there and then, a note in the branch record book. This will be sufficient. Or, if he has no qualms as to the attitude of Mr A, should he discover that enquiry has been made, he can obtain written confirmation. If, how-ever, he is utterly convinced of the good faith of Mr A he can accept his word. The forms would normally cover the Bank in all respects (except for the £450 mentioned previously), but he would be open to much practical and justified local criticism if it eventuated that A was lying, for it would be Mr G who suffered. The Defence Bonds pur-chased may well be withdrawn.

If no mention is made of the guarantor's reimbursement, the practical grounds for enquiry are much greater. Few customers could take ex-ception and most bankers would seek confirmation. If Mr G had not been repaid, the banker would wish to make the surplus policies monies available to him as guarantor. The forms could still cover the bank, but the criticism, in the event, of the bank having to resort to its legal rights would be greater. So, almost invariably, the banker would raise the question, if there was no mention in the letter. In fact, it is only when there is an oversight that any other course is likely to occur in practice, in instances when the letter makes no mention of the position of Mr G.

4 : A bankrupt guarantor

A bank takes a joint and several guarantee in the usual form from four persons. On the day on which it is signed by them a receiving order is made against one of the parties and he is subsequently adjudged bankrupt. Later it becomes necessary to call up the guarantee and the other three guarantors attempt to avoid liability on the grounds that as the receiving order took effect prior to the signing of the guarantee the document is completely invalidated. Advise the bank.

The first point to bear in mind is that a receiving order in bankruptcy operates from the commencement of the day on which it is made. Thus, since the guarantee is signed on the day on which the receiving order is made, the particular debtor, who later becomes bankrupt, is never at any time liable on the guarantee. This fact stems from Section 30, Sub-Section (3) of the Bankruptcy Act :

Save as aforesaid, all debts and liabilities, present or future, certain or contingent, to which the debtor is subject at the date of the receiving order, or to which he may become subject before his discharge by reason of any obligation incurred before the date of the receiving order, shall be deemed to be debts provable in bankruptcy.

The other basic principle is that where a number of persons enter into a contract on the understanding that an additional person is also going to enter into the contract, and for any reason that particular person does not enter into the contract, then the other persons have no responsibility. The point is illustrated in relation to a guarantee in the case of the *National Provincial Bank of England* v. *Brackenbury* (1906) 22 T.L.R. 797 :

A guarantee to a bank for an overdraft was, on its face, intended to be a joint and several guarantee by four guarantors. Three out of the four signed the guarantee, but the fourth did not sign, though willing to do so, and then died. It was held that the three who signed were not liable to the bank on the guarantee.

It will be noticed that in the above case the particular person had died. It is true that there is a difference between the example given and the question in that the particular guarantor, who subsequently became bankrupt, in fact signed the document. Nevertheless he was in law never at any time liable if one regards the receiving order as having been operative from the commencement of the day. It is this particular situation that gives rise to the practical and legal difficulty. In other words, the question of whether the actual signature, ineffective though it may be, is valid, is the point on which the decision would turn. On the principle that all concerned accepted the presumption of the liability of four joint and several guarantors, there is much to be said for the view that the remaining three could not be held to be liable. If, for example, someone holding a power of attorney had signed a guarantee after the donor had died, presumably the three remaining guarantors would still be able to escape liability. There would undoubtedly be not unsubstantial arguments to the contrary. Nevertheless it is submitted that the probabilities are fairly strong that the bank could not claim under such guarantee.

This view, however, has to be considered in the practical situation. In particular it is indicated that it is later that it becames necessary to call on the guarantors. If any of the three guarantors knowing of the receiving order acknowledges the debt to the bank, including perhaps even oral communications, they may well be estopped from denying that their liability continued notwithstanding the fact that the bankrupt debtor was not bound.

Another aspect at which one looks is the principle that where a receiving order has not been gazetted there is a certain amount of protection from Section 4 of the Bankrutcy Amendment Act, 1926. This, however, relates only to payment made for the bankrupt before the receiving order is gazetted. Here there is no payment made for the bankrupt. The payment is made for a third party on the expectation of the bankrupt remaining liable.

The solution is the inclusion in a bank guarantee form of a clause, which has been adopted in some instances, by which a number of guarantors signing a guarantee agree that they are bound notwithstanding the fact that one – or perhaps more – of their intended number does not complete the document. This clause may be in the terms that the bank may release any one of the four without releasing the others. The question would then depend on the interpretation of the actual clause itself.

Part five : Banker and customer

The fact that the banker and customer are in contractual relationship gives the position a greater flexibility than would be the position if the relationship were merely that of debtor and creditor. As is well-known, a banker–unlike an agent or a trustee–may use money, taken from his customers to form credit balances, for any purpose that the banker wishes so long as he honours his obligation to repay the money or pay it away in accordance with the customer's instructions, normally given in the form of a cheque. Inevitably there are a number of implied terms and the indications, encouraged by bank advertisements, are that these implied and ancillary functions are likely to increase. During the past ten years additional services have tended to become part of the contract by reason of advertisement, although other innovations are a matter of discretion in particular instances, such as the availability of cheque cards, rather that flowing from the relationship of banker and customer.

As to the questions:

Question 1

The repayment of an overdraft on demand is a term that is seldom enforced unless a customer is in breach of contract and thus bankers' arrangements for a facility for a period of months are regarded as effective. There is, however, no doubt that the banker can demand repayment without notice, although a course of dealing to the contrary may affect the position. Much has been added to this subject by reason of comments in a long judgment in a case (*Williams & Glyn's* v. *Barnes* (1980 – not yet reported). The obligation to repay on demand obtains generally but may easily be eliminated by what the banker may say to the customer. In addition the Unfair Contract Terms Act 1977, which did not apply to the Williams & Glyn's case because it stemmed from events prior to the operation of the Act, gives rights to a party where a contract is on the standard form of the other party and the effect is not what the first party might reasonably expect. How this Act will be applied depends very much on the discretion of the courts.

Question 2

This question illustrates the practical complication that bank managers usually overcome so satisfactorily by tact and practical ability.

Question 3
This question deals with the all too frequent consequence of mistakes. Sometimes it is a very far cry to recover money, despite the fact that there is a legal obligation on a third party to reimburse the bank.
Question 4
This has a very practical ring and may be helpful.
Question 5
This is a question concerning the fate of cheques and deals with a tender subject in that misunderstanding can arise so easily.
Question 6
This relates to the obligation not to answer status enquiries and deals with an unusual subject that would administratively disturb most chief accountants and chief inspectors if it ever became at all frequent.
Question 7
Probably the most difficult subject in banking law is the clash between the obligation of the customer to repay on demand and the obligation of the bank not to cut off a banking facility capriciously. (See also note to Question 1 above.)
Question 8
Here is an intriguing question and, it is thought, a good answer. One aspect, however, namely the liability of X Limited, is novel.
Question 9
Again, on bankers' enquiries, it is felt that there is little sympathy for judgment creditors making enquiries in order to ascertain whether they may garnishee monies and the result will not prompt much sympathy from banking circles.
Question 10
Since the answer was published there has been a further case which has confirmed the principle of *Garnett* v. *McKewan*. This case was that of *Halesowen Presswork & Assemblies Ltd* v. *Westminster Bank Ltd.* (*The Bankers' Magazine*, Dec. 1969, Sept. and December 1970). It has been confirmed in the House of Lords – 1972. A.C. 875.
Question 11
The essence of this answer is the need for effective notice of banking clearing arrangements to be given, but there is no question of any restriction upon the extent to which there can be such alterations.
Question 12
Mental incapacity gives rise to much more embarrassment for Branch Managers than need be the case. To a large extent this very good answer will provide the basis of practical advice.

1 : An overdraft repayable on demand

*Mr A has accounts at two different banks. At one of these an
overdraft limited was agreed and he received a letter from the bank
confirming the limit 'subject to the usual banking terms and
conditions'. Mr A enquired of both his bank managers precisely
what was meant by this phrase and was intrigued to find that there
was some diversity of opinion. What are these 'usual banking terms
and conditions' and any special significance which attaches to them?*

There is of course no doubt that all forms of charge taken by bankers
allude to repayment being on demand. It is also true that bankers
would readily testify that by their 'usual terms' they understand that
repayment is on demand. As the winning answer indicated, the nature
of deposit banking involving liquidity in theory necessitates such immediate repayment. That most bankers will admit that the borrowing of
some customers becomes a 'hard core' does not detract from the general
principle. Recently one or two banks have indicated their willingness,
within limited amounts, to lend on a 'term' basis, for perhaps two or
three years, in contradistinction to the normal basis.

This does not mean that the legal position is settled. In fact it is
probably one of the most difficult of the unresolved serious problems
of banking law today. Paget's *Law of Banking* (7th ed., p. 121) states :

It is generally assumed that temporary advances are repayable on
demand. How far this militates against the right of the customer not
to have his account closed except after reasonable notice, where the
advance is by way of overdraft, is not clear.

There may be one or two acceptable reconciliations of the principle
that a banker cannot capriciously and peremptorily decline to continue an overdraft but yet may demand repayment. On a rather artificial
basis it may be thought that the inability to dishonour cheques suddenly is not inconsistent with the right of the banker to ask for
repayment forthwith. In fact it is the need to avoid the sudden dishonour of cheques already drawn, and perhaps those drawn later from

pre-existing commitments, that is said to justify the clause in bank guarantee forms requiring notice of termination from the guarantor. Again, it may be suggested that the borrowing contract by implication, as essential to implement the intentions of the parties, necessitates such notice, it being further thought that such an implied principle overrides, as far as is necessary, the requirement of repayment on demand. Yet, while this contention is feasible where the term is customary, it is much more difficult, if not impossible, where there is a stipulation for repayment on demand in the form of charge taken over securities. There are however two Scottish cases (*Johnston* v. *Commercial Bank of Scotland* (1858, 2D, 790) and *Ritchie* v. *Clydesdale* (1886, 13R, 866)) that, although not dealing with the matter in much detail, touch in passing on the right of the customer to have notice of the termination of a facility which may be quite different from closing an account.

Probably the reason that the point has not been litigated is primarily the reluctance of the banker to exercise what appears to be a legal right. In most cases when the circumstances are such as to cause the bank to call in an overdraft there will have been a fundamental change in the customer's position, or perhaps a revelation of an inaccuracy in the information given at the time the overdraft was arranged, which will enable the banker to justify legally the termination of the facility quite apart from his right to have an advance repaid on demand.

2 : Husband's and wife's securities in one deed box

Mr A, a man of some means, has a joint account at the XYZ Bank Ltd with his wife; either party is authorised to sign cheques and also to deposit and withdraw securities, the bank holding its usual form of mandate.

There are securities held both in joint names and in individual names; there is also a locked deed box in safe custody held in joint names.

One day the bank receives a written request from Mr A, asking it to confirm that it will be prepared to release any of the securities held or the deed box upon request from either party at any time; in addition it should also be prepared to release these items, if so authorised, by the surviving party, should the other die.

Can the XYZ Bank Ltd agree to Mr A's request and if so would it be in order to give its confirmation in writing to its customer

Mr A's request entails consideration of five possible transactions:
(1) *The release of his securities to him.*
(2) *The release of Mrs A's securities to her.*
(3) *The release of his securities to her.*
(4) *The release of her securities to him.*
(5) *The release of securities (this including, for the moment, the Deed Box) in their joint names to either one of them.*

While both Mr A and his wife are living, these present little problem. The bank's duty is to see that whenever they part with a security, they do so either to the person on whose behalf they are holding it – the circumstances of the first two transactions – or, if held on behalf of more than one person, to all of them jointly, or to third parties in accordance with an authority received from the owner, or from all of the joint owners. Thus a suitably-worded authority signed by both Mr and Mrs A is required to enable the bank to meet their customers' wishes in respect of transactions of the other three classes.

The authority must relate specifically to securities held on behalf of the customers, and it is important to note that the mandate for either to draw cheques on the joint bank account cannot be taken to extend to the release of securities, *etc.* held in joint names. The authority should also be clear on the following matters :

(1) It must be unlimited as to time, not restricted by implication or otherwise to a single occasion.

(2) it must apply to securities to be deposited in the future, or it may have to be construed as applying only to those held by the bank on the date of the authority;

(3) it must allow either party to deal with securities, etc. in the sole name of the other or in their joint names; and

(4) as regards the Deed Box, the authority should cover withdrawals from and additions to the contents of the box, not merely access to it.

It is to be stressed that every mandate is dependent on its precise terms.

All these points will be covered by the bank's 'usual form of mandate' for the release of securities, but bankers will not need to be reminded of the basic rule that mandates are cancelled by the death of the giver of the mandate or, if there be more than one, of any of them. It therefore follows that, if the authority held by the XYZ Bank is no more than a simple mandate, they will have to tell Mr A that, after the death of one them, they will be able to release to the survivor only the securities held in his or her sole name, the instructions of the legal personal representatives being required in connection with those of the deceased, with the survivor joining in as well for those which were deposited jointly.

Some forms have been modified in recent years, however, to recognise the *fact* that while an agency is always cancelled by death, a contract of bailment *may* not be. The change from one to another is made simply by adding a clause to the effect that the authority shall not be revoked by the death of any of the parties giving it but shall continue to be effective until specifically revoked by any of the parties or by the legal personal representatives of a deceased party. It is important to note that such a modified form can have the effect only in relation to the kind of discharge the bank gets and could not in any way affect the devolution of the beneficial interest in the property.

The bank's reply to Mr A's enquiry must thus first take account of the precise nature of the authority they hold, and no doubt, if it is only a simple mandate, they will advise him what can be done to meet his wishes; but they are asked also to confirm that they will be prepared to release the security or the deed box upon request at any time.

It is possible that the securities, or some of them, now held or to be received in the future, may be in the bank's hands in such circumstances that they could establish a lien over them, but they would be unable to do this in the face of their own letter confirming their preparedness to release them on request at any time; they will thus wish to consider the advisability of adding a suitable qualification in respect of any items, whether or not the subject of a charge to the bank, of which they might wish to be entitled to retain possession. Much more could be said on the topic of lien, particularly in relation to the contents of the deed box, but this is perhaps not the place for it to be considered in detail. A deed box, like any other chattel, is different from a share certificate which, if registered in the joint names and deposited in joint names, can be delivered to the survivor. With a deed box, unless there is a bailment agreement as indicated above, the authority of the personal representatives of the deceased is always required, as well as that of the other joint holder.

There is one further point which requires consideration before the bank's reply is drafted, since what has so far been said assumes that Mr and Mrs A are the beneficial owners of the items held by the bank. If, however, there is any element of trusteeship, of which the bank has notice, in their ownership of any of them, then, so far as those items are concerned, all the parties must be governed by the provisions of current trustee legislation and the trust deed, if there is one, and it may be that the bank will find it cannot agree to its customer's request.

3 : An incorrect bank statement

A bank has two customers – P. Smith and B. Smith (whose signatures are very much alike). On 7 January 1965 P. Smith makes a cheque out for £30 for his account and in error on the 14 January 1965 it is debited to B. Smith's account

On 14 August P. Smith dies, up to which date no bank statements have been sent out. The wife of P. Smith, shortly after thinking that the account is in order and having received probate (and being the sole beneficiary), draws off the balance. On 16 November B. Smith has his statement from the bank and does not notice the debit for £30 as the cheque was not included with his statement. On 24 December B. Smith realises that the £30 has been debited in error and informs the bank.

Should the bank recredit B's account and obtain the £30 from P's wife? What rights has the bank against P's wife?

Clearly this problem falls into two parts : that relating to the position of the bank as between B. Smith, whose account the bank incorrectly debited with the £30 on 14 January and that between the bank and Mrs. P. Smith, the widow of the account holder whose account should have been debited with the £30 on 14 January.

As between the bank and Mr. B. Smith there is no doubt whatsoever that the bank is under a duty to recredit his account. Quite apart from the law relating to the return by a customer of a passbook or a bank statement, the situation is such that the customer was entitled to the further monies. In fact the main concern for the bank would be as to whether cheques drawn on his account by Mr B. Smith had been dishonoured in the meantime. In all probability this was not so because otherwise had cheques been drawn on the strength of the true balance the incorrect item debited would have come to light before the discovery on 24 December 1965, which, according to the question, is the date on which Mr B. Smith realised that £30 had been debited to his account in error and told the bank. Had, however, the bank dishonoured such cheques drawn in the interim period there is no doubt that they would have been liable for damages if the dishonouring of the cheques had been consequent upon the wrongful debiting of the £30. In fact, even if a cheque had been dishonoured because there was, say, a shortage on the account to the extent of £35, there might have been damage arising in that it could have been alleged that had there been a shortage of only £5 the bank would not have returned cheques. This would in part depend as to whether there was evidence as to the customer having overdrawn his account previously for a very small amount. Fortunately, however, in the case in question this aspect has not arisen.

The law relating to the significance of the return of a passbook or statement is well known. In fact there is no doubt that whilst entries may be *prima facie* evidence in favour of bankers, they are also *prima facie* evidence against them. In the case of *Commercial Bank of Scotland* v. *Rhind* (1860) 3 Macq. 643 at p. 648, Lord Campbell, who was then Lord Chancellor, said:

It would indeed be a reproach of the law of Scotland, if, there being satisfactory evidence that, by the mistake of a clerk, there had been in the pass book a double entry of the same sum to the credit of the respondent, the mistake could in no way be shown by the bank, and if he were entitled fraudulently to extort from them £80 beyond the amount of what is justly due to him.

He then went to on to indicate that:

. . . on proof of its (the pass book's) having been in the custody of the customer, and returned by him to the bankers without objection being made to any of the entries by which the bankers are credited, I think such entries may be *prima facie* evidence for the bankers as those on the other side are *prima facie* evidence against them.

The case of *Holland* v. *Manchester and Liverpool District Banking Co. Ltd.* (1909) 25 T.L.R. 386, is also indicative of the position arising in the question, although that case related to an overpayment. This brings us to the other aspect, that of the relationship between the bank and Mrs P. Smith, who was the widow and sole beneficiary of Mr P. Smith, who died on 14 August. The general law, as indicated in the above two cases, is that if a person has altered his position upon the strength of being wrongly credited with an amount (or possibly by reason of not having been debited with an amount that should have been charged to his account) then the money cannot be claimed back from him by the bank. Naturally, however, where an amount is of significant size the court will be jealous in accepting the contention of a customer that he had presumed that an amount received and credited to his account was due to him or that an amount not in fact debited to his account had in fact been debited. In fact, in the latter instance, which is the case with which we are dealing, the burden of proof on the customer would appear to be greater. Where someone has drawn a cheque for a particular sum then he will know that sometimes it may be months before the cheque is debited to the account. Nevertheless, where perhaps six months has ensued he would expect all cheques to have been charged, or that they would have been returned to him for confirmation. All this, however, is not a question of law, it is a question of evidence and the extent to which the truthfulness of what the customer says, and as to his state of mind, is or is not accepted.

With the case of Mrs Smith unfortunately Mr Smith is dead and it is not possible to consider the particular aspect as to his belief. Moreover, Mrs Smith will not have been credited with the knowledge of cheques that had been drawn unless it can be substantiated that counterfoils of the cheques issued were available to her. Again, as the correspondent emphasised, it is possible for an executrix to give notice that all debts are to be notified. If that notice is given then the executrix as such has a right to distribute the estate. This does not, however, mean that an item cannot be followed. The recent case of *Re Diplock, Diplock* v. *Wintle* 1948 Ch. 465 definitely illustrated the extent to which this could be pursued. In that instance large sums had been paid over to charities and to the extent, in very broad terms, that they had not been utilised and could be traced, such as into the charity's banking account, then the items were recoverable.

Thus, so far as Mrs Smith is concerned, if she could have established, as might well be the case, that she had altered her position and utilised the £30, then it would not be recoverable by the bank. If the estate of the late Mr Smith had been very small, the expenditure of the money would have been easy to establish. On the other hand, if his estate had been £1,000 or more in law the bank would have had a good prospect of effecting recovery, although the practical circumstances of the death and the widowhood would disincline them to pursue the matter formally. There is no doubt, however, that they will have to recredit the account of Mr B. Smith with the sum of £30 with which he was debited in error.

4 : Chattels of the fugitive customer

A lady, indebted to the bank in the sum of £50, and does not answer letters asking for repayment; she appears to have left her last known address.

Through the post there arrives a parcel addressed to her, care of the bank. Enquiry from the suppliers elicits the information that the parcel contains a gift to her, from a friend, of diamonds worth £250.

Can the bank (i) refuse to hand over the parcel to the customer, should she call, until the overdraft has been cleared, and (ii) at the end of, say, three months, if the position is still the same, sell the diamonds and credit the proceeds to her account?

It may be that the essence of the problem was overshadowed by the relatively small amounts involved. All the instincts of the practical banker are to avoid criticisms, if not possible legal vulnerability, likely to result if he followed either of the courses contemplated in the question. However an answer, whilst quite properly alluding to the dominant practical considerations, should deal with the fundamental legal problem as if much larger sums were involved – so large in fact that the banker would need to do all possible to recoup himself. The problem was retained in the form submitted, without altering the figures, as it was thought that the relatively small sums presented a further facet of the case rather than a method by which the intrinsic points could be avoided.

The essential point is that indebtedness of the customer upon whom demand for payment has been made unsuccessfully by the banker. In addition the banker has received a parcel addressed to the customer care of the banker, the contents of which are understood to be worth far more than the debt.

The first legal question is as to the basis upon which the parcel is held by the banker. Is it the same as if it had been deposited in safe custody? Or is it in a different category because it has been sent to the banker without previous agreement? If the bank has received similar parcels previously then the customer is entitled to have them looked after in the same way as before. If for example the banker has previously issued a safe custody receipt to the customer on receipt of

G

parcels of diamonds then his obligations will be the same in the present instance. If, however, it is an isolated instance then the mere receipt by the banker of the parcel does not place him in the same position as if he were undertaking safe custody. Now safe custody excludes the suggestion of a lien beyond all doubt. Where there is no safe custody arrangement that the customer can establish however, the right of a creditor to retain property belonging to his debtor is not automatic. It can arise as a common law lien, such as where the money is owed for work done on the chattel or where the party by reason of his position is obliged to receive the items such as a carrier or an innkeeper, or where a maritime lien arises, for example, in respect of the cost of salvaging goods. Otherwise, a 'general' lien to hold for *all* debts, such as a solicitors' or factors' or bankers' lien, arises because of the customary implications of the relationship between the parties. A bankers' lien extends to negotiable securities, probably to a life policy but probably not to deeds (see *re Bowes* (1886) 33 *Ch.D.* 586). Certainly it would not appear to extend to chattels. So that the banker has no right to retain the diamonds.

Should he refuse to hand them over he is liable for conversion. Now normally the measure of damage will be no more than the value of the diamonds. It may be that they will be subject to a contract for sale involving a profit that cannot be completed, but this is unlikely in the circumstances. This means that in all probability the banker would suffer little despite his refusal to deliver the parcel since he has the diamonds. Meanwhile, his solution is to sue his customer for the debt. When the judgment is obtained and remains unsatisfied he can seek satisfaction by issuing execution against the diamonds by the same procedure as an unpaid judgment creditor seizes the furniture of his debtor (a write of *fi. fa.*). After seizure and advertisement the goods are sold and used to repay the debt of the unsatisfied creditor.

As to the suggestion of selling at the end of three months, this too would be a conversion and the damage may be more than the proceeds of sale. In *Sachs* v. *Miklos* (1948) 2 *K.B.* 23 the claim by a depositary of goods to sell as an agent of necessity where the owner could not be found was held to be bad and the defendant liable for conversion. So would be the banker in the case envisaged except that he would have a cross-claim for his debt and the balance of the proceeds of sale, which may or may not be enough. He would also be likely to have to pay the costs.

98

5 : Enquiry as to fate of
cheque tendered for a third party credit

*Mr X pays in at the XYZ Bank, Anytown Branch, for the
credit of his account with the ABC Bank, a crossed cheque
drawn on the XYZ Bank, Anytown Branch and demands to
know if the cheque is paid.*

*What is the position of the XYB Bank assuming: (a) the ABC
Bank is local; (b) the ABC Bank is not local; (c) there is no
local branch of the ABC Bank.*

*Would the position be any different if Mr X was a customer at
another branch of XYZ Bank?*

Part of this question has often been canvassed at meetings but the
variations contained in the form in which it was submitted by our
correspondent raise several new aspects. Throughout it must be remembered that as between a paying banker and a third party crossed cheques
may be paid only to another banker and also that the paying banker
(and indirectly his customer) has until the close of business to dishonour such a cheque presented in the ordinary course (*i.e.*, through
the post or the clearing) by another banker. The only exception is
the special presentation when a clerk of the collecting banker physically presents a cheque. Then it is the obligation of the paying banker
to give an answer. Although there has not been a decided case on the
point, if the banker does not immediately pay a cheque presented
over the counter by another banker, the cheque is dishonoured. Failure
to pay immediately is dishonour. Where, as sometimes may happen
in practice, the presenting banker agrees to wait, there is probably
still dishonour, strictly speaking, in that payment is not made immediately; however, the 're-presentation' a few hours later frequently
overcomes embarrassment (and possible litigation) that might otherwise ensue. The other fact to be considered in answering the problem
is that an opinion regarding a customer is given only to another banker.

There are four questions :

(*a*) X pays in a cheque at the drawee bank for the credit of his
account at a local bank and wishes to know whether the cheque is
paid. This is *not* special presentation, which can come only through

a clerk of the collecting bank. (Incidentally, if this were not so, banking would cease to be a practical proposition.) The drawee bank certainly has the whole day in which to give an answer to the ABC Bank to whom Mr X should be referred. Contractually, even, the XYZ Bank (that is the drawee bank) could send the cheque to the ABC Bank where the account is kept. It would confirm that the bank was willing to collect. Such a course would be artificial and impractical, but it is very doubtful whether damages could be claimed. Where the branch of the bank on which the cheque is drawn is local the bank where the payee keeps his account could easily specially present the cheque as soon as it came into their hands and a modicum of intelligence on the part of Mr X would lead him to deliver the cheque at his own bank locally and request that it be specially presented. There may be an implied or a customary right for a customer to insist on having a cheque presented specially, but it is apparent that this cannot be in an unlimited number of instances, for otherwise banking could not function. Such an implied term would not be necessary to the business efficacy of the contract (the test of a truly implied term): in fact it would make business impossible. Similarly a custom must be reasonable, which a right to demand an unlimited number of special presentations would not be. In practice a customer making an unreasonable number of requests would probably be asked to take his account elsewhere – a solution that a banker can (and does) pursue occasionally without having to give any reason, thus obviating litigation that might otherwise occur.

(b) Where the branch is not local Mr X would not have the above opportunity.

(c) For this purpose there is little if any difference between Mr X's Bank – the ABC Bank – being a local bank and a bank having a local branch. Where there is any branch or head office of his own bank, a clerk of that institution may make a special presentation whether or not he is employed at the branch where the account is kept. In fact special presentations are generally effective through local branches of the collecting bank or through its head office. The only requirement is that any relevant clearing house or local clearing rules must not be flouted.

If Mr X pays in a cheque for the credit of his account at another branch of the XYZ Bank and not for an account at another bank the position is much more difficult. There is no doubt that, subject to the above observation regarding the number of occasions on which special presentations can be requested, the XYZ Bank could not decline to effect notionally a special presentation if Mr X insisted on communicating directly or indirectly with the branch where he kept his account. The drawee branch cannot refuse to act after instructions. At least it is difficult to see how they could defend an action by Mr X and it is also difficult to see on what grounds the drawer could criticise the bank for paying or returning the cheque. A customer of a bank is entitled to the benefit of a special presentation effected through another branch (even although it is the drawee branch). The alternatives (*b*) and (*c*) obviously are not applicable if XYZ Bank is the drawee bank.

6 : Agreeing not to answer status enquiries

Mr A is an influential customer of Lowtown Bank Ltd who has informed his manager that he does not wish the bank to answer status enquiries on his account because he has reason to believe his nephew is seeking to obtain information regarding his personal affairs.

Shortly afterwards the manager receives two enquiries from other branches of Lowtown Bank Ltd. The first enquiries whether Mr A is a suitable person to introduce a current account customer, the second as to his sufficiency for £5,000 in the way of business.

The manager, unable to contact Mr A who is on holiday, replies to both enquiries in favourable terms, but a week later is informed by Mr A that the fact that the replies have been made has come to his notice, and he threatens to sue the bank for damages because of a 'breach of secrecy'.

What is the position of Lowtown Bank Ltd, and would it be different if the enquiries had been received from another bank and replied to in similar terms?

The first point occurring to the practical banker is whether an account would be opened on this basis. To make such an arrangement in one instance might be attractive if the business were particularly valuable. However, the thought of a number of customers having accounts with the stipulation that no replies were to be made to status enquiries would be administratively an unwarranted, if not an unmanageable, problem. It would mean that when a new member of the staff – a relief manager for example – took up duty he would have to be told of the existence of a number of accounts about which information is not to be disclosed. It would also mean that warning notices would have to be inserted on many internal documents and files. All too frequently enquiries come by telephone from other banks and branches and, sooner or later, disclosure is likely to happen. Secondly, if a banker decided to permit such an arrangement exceptionally, he would be wise to agree with the customer the terms in which such enquiries are refused. The answer might otherwise be confused with the banker being 'unable to speak for the figures quoted', which is commonplace.

There is also the legal aspect. Where someone does business with, for example, a stockbroker he may be regarded as binding himself to the established practices of that business. If one deals in a particular market one is taken to have accepted this implication. Where a banking account is opened, the banker has an obligation of secrecy without there being any special arrangement. This obligation is subject to exceptions, summarised conveniently in the case of *Tournier* v. *National Provincial Bank and Union Bank of England* [1924] 1 K.B. 461). One of these exceptions is the implied consent. It has not been specifically held that this consent follows automatically as a part of the usage between banker and customer. It is thought and generally accepted that there would be no difficulty in establishing the point unless the customer could establish that he was unaware of the practice – a very unlikely contingency. Most writers appear to regard it as beyond contention and there is certainly no judicial comment to the contrary. What comment there is supports the view. Because, however, there is an unwritten term in a contract it does not mean that it cannot be eliminated. If the customer requests that no enquiries be answered and the banker thereafter opens or continues the account there is no doubt that the stipulation forms a term of the contract. By answering the enquiry the banker is in breach of his contractual obligation.

A right to claim more than nominal damage does not follow automatically from a breach of contract. The loss consequent upon the breach has to be proved. It must not be too remote, in that it must have been a consequence that would be expected to follow from such a breach, either generally or having regard to any special knowledge of which the party committing the breach is aware or of which he should have been aware.

Upon the foregoing principles one must decide whether the bank is in breach of contract and if so what loss may have been caused and is also claimable. That a person is of such a standing as justifies the opening of a current account is information of so ordinary a character that its wrongful disclosure could hardly cause damage. The reply nevertheless confirms the information that Mr A has an account at the Lowtown Bank. It is just possible that this knowledge could give rise to loss by enabling a judgment creditor to know where to try to enforce a judgment order by serving a garnishee order, but with a

103

customer of the standing of Mr A such a view may not be relevant. The reply relating to £5,000 on the other hand may give the nephew information that may prove a practical embarrassment. The nephew may wish to borrow and Mr A may find it much more difficult to decline because the nephew knows of his worth. This is something that a court may be willing to measure in money although the amount would not be very great. One may envisage perhaps other circumstances, but these must not be such that Mr A had a legal obligation to disclose in any event.

The fact that information reaches a third party is the point that is material. Whether it takes place through another branch or another bank does not affect the position unless the knowledge of the other bank itself operated to the detriment of the customer. With the other branch this could not possibly give rise to any claims unless information is passed to a third party.

7 : Commitments and outstanding cheques after demand for repayment

X Limited, who are traders with a seasonal business, has a facility from its bankers of £50,000 for the purpose of its trade. The bank has security of a legal mortgage of freehold property worth £20,000. The bank manager has become dissatisfied with a number of aspects of the customer's business and makes demand for repayment. The customer contends that (a) the bank must pay outstanding cheques, and (b) must meet outstanding commitmetns into which the company has entered upon the presumption of the continuance of the overdraft facility.

Has the company a right of action against the bank if (i) cheques outstanding are dishonoured and (ii) if cheques drawn in respect of the above-mentioned commitments are dishonoured?

Briefly this problem poses the dilemma between the obligation of a bank's customer to repay indebtedness to it on demand and the banker's policy of not suddenly cutting off facilities to his customer. How these conflicting aspects of banking practice may be reconciled is the basic point of this problem.

The basis upon which bank indebtedness is repayable on demand rests, of course, on the premise that the bank has to repay depositors at short notice – a feature more in evidence in the last century than today. The evidence of this obligation to repayment on demand is stated on almost every bank form of security; there is no doubt about it. In cases where there is no security there would be no difficulty in establishing that this obligation is the customary basis of bank borrowing. Bank managers often write letters to their customers reminding them that their indebtedness is repayable on demand; if not, they will almost always at least refer to the advance being 'on the usual banking terms'.

In spite of this right, however, few bankers would, entirely without fear as to the consequences legally or otherwise, peremptorily terminate overdraft facilities. They are aware that customers have commitments; and they are aware that cheques will have to be issued on the strength of the continuance of the overdraft.

This point has been seldom (relatively) a matter of legal controversy, in fact probably because banks do not capriciously demand repayment of borrowing. Usually when demand is made the customer himself will have received plenty of notice and warning of the bank's dissatisfaction. Moreover, the customer is probably likely himself to be in breach of contract with the bank, which would stultify any contention that he might be able to put forward that the termination of the facility is also in breach.

This subject has not gone unnoticed in legal text books. The best summary of the position is that in *Banking Law* (8th edn.), (London: Wallace and McNeil, 1949), p. 19, quoted below. (Incidentally, although this is a book on banking law in Scotland there is no suggestion that the law on the subject under discussion differs from that obtaining in England):

"Where a banker has permitted his customer to overdraw his account with or without security, his having done so in the past does not preclude his refusing to continue to do so in the future. The banker may, without assigning any reason, intimate that he declines to allow any further overdrafts on the account, and may call upon the customer and his sureties (if any) to make immediate provision for the liquidation of the debt. Where a customer has been allowed to overdraw against security, the banker is under no obligation to continue facilities until the security is exhausted, and where no special period has been stipulated for he may at any time refuse to cash his customer's cheques and call for repayment. This rule is, however, modified to the extent that the banker must not act with undue harshness towards his customer, and if such customer has in the past been allowed to overdraw his account against security a banker is liable in damages if in similar circumstances with the same customer he, without reasonable notice, dishonours a cheque."

On the face of the matter the overriding legal position appears to be that bank indebtedness is repayable on demand. Cases relating to the ability of a bank to terminate suddenly a facility are not of tremendous help. The first, *Johnston* v. *Commercial Bank* (1858) 20 D 790, was a Scottish case relating to a bond of cash credit. The normal bond of cash credit obliges the customer to pay on demand sums owing. In that case it was suggested that the bank had arbitrarily terminated the facility in that they were making demand. A lord justice stated 'I do not say that there may not be a case for damage when a bank without good cause capriciously stops advancing without notice'.* However, in that particular case more security had been requested and it was considered that the circumstances provided notice. This was, of course, quite an old case. In the case of *Ritchie* v. *Clydesdale Bank* (1886) 13 R 866, the position was somewhat similar but here it was indicated quite emphatically that there was no contract to provide credit on an indefinite basis. Perhaps of most recent pertinence is the case of *Buckingham* v. *Midland Bank Ltd.* (1895) 12 TLR. Here there was a loan account and a credit account; and it was held as a question of fact that reasonable notice should have been given to terminate the loan account facility. This was, however, slightly different in that cheques drawn on a credit current account balance had been dishonoured. In the course of evidence given as to fact, two senior bank officials indicated that there was no custom by which a banker had to give notice. It seems, however, that that evidence was not accepted.

The solution may perhaps well be that demand may in certain circumstances imply a reasonable time. Undoubtedly, with a bill of exchange or promissory note, payment on demand means payment immediately. With, however, other demands in other connections it has been suggested that reasonable time must be given. Another and possible way of reconciling the position is that a bank cannot without notice close the banking account; it cannot terminate the facility and, therefore, cannot refuse to pay cheques without some reasonable notice, if the customer is not in default; but nevertheless the customer is under a legal obligation to repay what is previously borrowed.

Probably, indebtedness is always repayable on demand; but there is an implied term that the customer's credit must not be damaged if it can be established that a period of notice is necessary to the business efficacy of the arrangement. A measure of confirmation of the above views is contained in the judgment in Williams & Glyn's v. Barnes (1980). See page 87 supra.

*See also Question (1) supra at page 89 The dictum of Herschell L. C. in *Rouse* v. *Bradford Banking Co.* (1894 A.C. 586 at page 595) also confirms the above principle.—ED.

8 : A banker's enquiry and mistaken identity

*X Ltd was inviting tenders for a large contract and one condition
of the tender was the supplying of bankers' names and addresses
by the companies tendering, for the purpose of bankers' inquiries.*

*A. B., Ltd. tendered for the contract and gave their bankers
as Z Bank Ltd, 895 Straight Street, Lowtown.*

*In due course Y Bank Ltd (the bankers of X Ltd) sent a banker's
inquiry re A. B. Ltd, no address given, to Z Bank Ltd, Straight
Street, Lowtown, the street number being omitted. This was delivered
to another branch of Z Bank Ltd in Straight Street, Lowtown,
which had an account in the name of A.B. (C) Ltd, a small
private, limited company. This bank was quite surprised at the
terms of the inquiry, which were for a £250,000 contract, and after
some hesitation decided to send the following reply: 'If your
inquiry refers to A. B. (C) Ltd., of 100 Diagonal Street, Lowtown,
the directors are respectable and trustworthy, but your amount
appears to be rather high in relation to the figures before us'.
What is the legal position if Y Bank Ltd failed to
pass on the condition to the detriment of X Ltd?*

It must be appreciated that a number of actions are being contemplated, or are possible :

(*i*) A. B. Ltd, who claim to have lost the contract through the events that have happened, may sue Y Bank Ltd, who were the bankers of the company inviting the tender for the contract.

(*ii*) A. B. Ltd may also sue X Ltd, who invited the tenders for the contract, on the grounds that it was Y Bank Ltd, the bankers of X Ltd, who omitted in informing their customers of the reply received the reference 'if your inquiry refers to A. B. (C) Ltd, 100 Diagonal Street, Lowtown .

(*iii*) A. B. (C) Ltd may consider bringing an action against its own bankers for giving unauthorised disclosure as to its affairs.

First, the general law relating to bankers opinions should be considered. On the one hand there is the question of the liability of the banker giving an opinion if that opinion eventuates to be inaccurate.

Until the Unfair Contract Terms Act 1977, that came into force in February 1978, the banks were protected from negligence by the standard clause excluding responsibility. That is to say: If they were negligent but honest they had no liability. Section 2 (2) provides that 'In the case of . . . loss or damage a person cannot so exclude or restrict his liability for negligence except insofar as the term of notice satisfies the requirement of reasonableness'. This could well make the reservation worthless. This position stems from the case of *Hedley Byrne & Co.* v. *Heller and Partners Ltd.* (1962) 1 QB 396 and (1963) 2 All ER 575. From a practical standpoint negligence would be difficult to establish because bankers customarily give answers (as illustrated from the above problem) in a euphemistic vernacular. Sometimes, however, as in the present instance, the failure to give a favourable answer when it should have been given will itself cause damage, especially as the delicacy of bankers' terms are known and now commercially assessed with more perspicuity.

Again there is also the question of whether bankers have an implied authority to answer opinions from other bankers without explicit authority. There is little doubt that they have this implied authority, where the customer of himself will be aware of the usage. It is just possible that where, say, an old lady, remote from banking affairs and commercial life, has no knowledge of the giving of banker's opinions she would be able to claim that there was no authority to disclose because the usage should be known to both parties. However, this is unlikely and unrealistic. As a third possibility one has to realise that persons with whom one is not in contractual relationship may have a responsibility either for negligence or libel. Negligence being a breach of duty owed by one person to another frequently occurs when, for example, someone crossing a road is knocked down by a car. Furthermore, it has been decided and was mentioned in the Hedley Byrne case that this duty is not limited to physical harm. Libel being the written form of defamation is often answered by the suggestion that there is a claim of privilege, namely that the comment was impliedly justified by the surrounding circumstances.

As to the first action, that is of A.B. Ltd. against Y Bank Ltd, there is no direct contractual relationship. It may be suggested that there is a duty to take care in the same way as accountants preparing a company's balance sheet have a duty, not only to the company but to third parties who may be expected to read the balance sheet, to take care. This point has never been before the courts in the particular circumstances. Y Bank Ltd could well have foreseen the consequences of their inaccuracy had they known it. That is to say, acting for a third party, their customer X Ltd, they pass on inaccurately and, in the circumstances, materially inaccurately, information relating to a third party. The issue has not been before the courts and probably if A.B. Ltd were bringing legal actions they would be advised to sue Y Bank Ltd direct. It is possible, but improbable, that the courts would extend the principle of *Hedley Byrne* to these circumstances, but from a practical standpoint it will be appreciated that it is not so far removed from the circumstances in which accountants may have a responsibility for an inaccuracy in a balance sheet, not only to their clients, but also to third parties who rely upon the representation. The action against Y might well succeed.

The second possibility is much more novel, namely that the company concerned whose bankers were at fault should be sued. In practice, of course, one has to realise that the proof of actual loss stemming from the circumstances would be extremely difficult. It would mean that the position was so blatant that X Ltd were unable to find any possible extraneous reason that would justify their rejecting the particular offer. The legal situation would not be affected by any contractual relationship because the offer was unaccepted. It would be dependent upon the position outside the realm of contract, namely in tort.

That is to say that there would be a right of action against X Ltd if there were a duty of care. The action would be based on the tort of negligence. On the basis of the *Hedley Byrne* principle, mentioned above, by making the offer X Ltd has put itself sufficiently in relationship to A. B. Ltd by inviting tenders. Therefore it would seem that in fact X Ltd is responsible if Y Bank Ltd acted as its agent. There seems to be no other explanation and thus the answer to this perhaps controversial point is that X Ltd are thought to be liable.

The question of the liability of A. B. (C) Ltd bankers to that company for giving unauthorised information is a more simple question. The answer was given in response to an ordinary banker's inquiry. That inquiry on the basis outlined earlier in this note is within the ambit of the banker/customer relationship and, therefore, the bank has no liability.

Thus, to summarise, A. B. Ltd may perhaps successfully sue Y Bank Ltd direct; they may also be able to sue X Ltd successfully; A. B. (C) Ltd has no claim against its banker.

110

9 : Full information on a banker's enquiry

*A firm of solicitors ask their bank, Bank A, to inquire of Branch X
of Bank B, whether a Mr F is good for £50 credit.*

*Branch X of Bank B have no account in the name of Mr F
but know he keeps an account at Branch X of Bank C.*

(i) What action should the branch of Bank B take?

*(ii) If Bank A receives a satisfactory reply to its inquiry from
X Branch of Bank C and not from Bank B, should Bank A when
passing on the reply to the solicitors mention that the reply has
been received from another bank?*

*(iii) Assuming that Bank A does not mention that the reply
has been received, in fact, from Bank C, is Bank A liable to its
customers if it later transpires that the solicitors when making their
original request were merely endeavouring to ascertain whether
Mr F maintained an account at the X Branch of Bank B, with
a view to the issue of a subpœna on that particular branch?*

The point B has to consider before replying is whether it should disclose
that Mr F keeps an account at Bank C. It is not its duty to enquire of
Bank C and then pass forward the reply to Bank A. In *Parsons* v.
Barclay & Co. Ltd. (1910) Cozens-Hardy M. R. is reported as saying
that

> ... he wished emphatically to repudiate the suggestion that when
> a banker was asked for a reference of this kind it was any part of his
> duty to make enquiries outside as to the solvency or otherwise of the
> person asked about, or to do more than answer the question put to him
> honestly from what he knew from the books and accounts before him.

The practice of bankers giving status opinions was referred to in the
following terms by Lord Morris of Borth-y-Gest in *Hedley Byrne & Co.
Ltd.* v. *Heller and Partners, Ltd.* (1963):

> ... the bank need not have answered the enquiry from the National
> Provincial Bank. It appears, however, that it is a matter of banking

convenience or courtesy and presumably of mutual business advantage that enquiries between banks will be answered.

Bank B should reply that it has no account in the name of Mr F. It is not obliged to let Bank A know that he keeps an account at Bank C; but as it is customary for bankers to be helpful on these occasions, it could add this fact to its reply.

Bank A should mention that the reply has been received from another bank, since if it fails to do so it will be reasonable for its customers, having expressly asked for the inquiry to be made of Bank B, to infer that the reply was given by that bank.

If a reply from Bank B is not satisfactory, as the question may imply – the bank being aware possibly of some adverse information concerning Mr F not known to Bank C – Bank A should not withhold this reply from its customers. The form of inquiry would lead it to suppose that its customers were contemplating a business transaction of £50 with Mr F rather than that, as subsequently appears, its customers were concerned only to establish the existence of an account in the name of Mr F at Bank B. It should be apparent to Bank A, therefore, that its customers may rely on the satisfactory reply and afford credit to Mr F, and that such credit might not be given if its customers were aware of the unsatisfactory reply from Bank B.

It is probable, however, that Bank B has not sent an unsatisfactory reply from the standpoint of reporting specifically unfavourably, but has merely indicated that it has no account. The approach to that bank is probably an error and would be of no practical significance unless the account had been closed in unfavourable circumstances, which information could be of interest to an inquirer.

The point here is whether the bank is liable on a claim for negligence, since the circumstances of the case make it seem unreasonable to suppose there was any question of fraud. In order to succeed on the grounds of negligence, a breach of duty would have to be proved.

A duty of care exists where there is a contractual or fiduciary relationship. The case of *Hedley Byrne & Co., Ltd.* v. *Heller & Partners, Ltd.*, dealt with the circumstances in which a duty of care arises when one banker gives an opinion to another bank at the request of a customer.

The position of Bank A, however, is that of a banker passing on to his own customer an opinion given by another banker. It was held in *Midland Bank* v. *Seymour* (1954) that

    . . . inquiries made by a bank on behalf of its customers, though made in the ordinary course of banking business, were made on a contractual basis as part of its services, and that a bank was under a duty, in passing on the result of such inquiries, not to supply misleading information.

It would appear that Bank A, in that its customers will have understood from the reply that Mr F maintains an account at Bank B, has given information capable of misleading, and that in doing so it was in breach of duty and so liable for any damage suffered by its customers.

The bank might submit (a) that the enquiry as put to it by its customers was not founded on a matter of £50 credit – if this is in fact so – and that to that extent it was misled as to the reason for the inquiry and (b) that if its customers wished to establish the existence of an account in the name of Mr F at Bank B, they should more properly have been asked to inquire of Bank B as to whether Mr F was good for his engagements – it being generally accepted that a bank would not express an opinion on a non-customer without making it clear that it does not have the account.

It is the normal practice of bankers not to quote the name of the bank supplying the opinion when passing it on to its customers. If Bank A followed this procedure, it might contend that it did not specify by name, that it was Bank C which gave the opinion, and that, in the absence of any confirmation, its customers were not fully justified in proceeding on the assumption that the opinion was, in fact, given by that particular bank. The instruction from the customers was, however, quite explicit : to inquire of Bank B; and although the bank did make the inquiry, it did not pass on the reply.

Thus to Summarise:

1. Perhaps the best course is to say 'account now with other bankers'. There is no obligation to do more. Alternatively with consent of the client or perhaps without, the enquiry could be sent on to the new bankers, provided that the answer is given as above. In practice the new bank is usually mentioned but the course is probably not entirely free from legal risk.

2. There is a duty to give information to a customer of the source of any information received.

H

3. The damage is likely to be small even if there were a liability arising from the misapprehension of the enquirers as to the bank and branch where the account is kept.

10 : Combining accounts

Blank Bank know that their customer Mr A is leaving the district
within a few days, if he has not already gone. He is £100 overdrawn
on current account, but has £300 on deposit account and the bank
is fully expecting cheques to be presented in excess of any available
balance. This has been a troublesome account, and the bank
is anxious to obtain £10 in charges.

Can the bank under advice to the customer's last known address
debit him immediately with the £10 charges and also amalgamate
his deposit account with the current account? This would leave
an available balance of £190 credit and Blank Bank would
wish to dishonour any cheques presented in excess of this balance.

It is clear that there are two distinct problems: the right of the bank
to combine the accounts and the right of the bank to debit its charges.

The right of a bank to combine accounts has long been a matter of
some controversy. In 1924 in the case of *Greenhalgh* v. *Union Bank
of Manchester,* Mr Justice Swift indicated that there was an implication that if two accounts were opened the bank undertook to keep them
separate in the absence of any other arrangement. However, that particular case concerned special facts; the better view is that it is a decision
resting on its facts and that the *dictum* mentioned above is similarly
subject to the particular facts not being of general application. The
view taken is that the case of *Garnett* v. *McKewan* (1872), which was a
case decided before the Court of Appeal, recapitulates the correct law.
Certainly Paget takes that view; and it seems that Lord Chorley inclines
to accept this view (see *Law of Banking* (5th edn.), 1967, p. 60). Unfortunately the opposite standpoint received some support in an article
in *The Journal of the Institute of Bankers* in 1925 (vol. XLV, p. 283);
but as this view has since been criticised continually by all the authori-
ties it is thought that a banker may combine two current accounts
without notice, unless one is a trust account. Certainly that policy has
been followed in practice fairly frequently, although there still remains
some controversy. It is accepted by all concerned that where there is
a loan account there is no such right to combine without notice. Other-

wise this would defeat the purpose of the arrangement. The decision of *Re E. J. Morel* (1934), *Ltd.* (1962) Ch. D.21, which concerned a stopped account that the court decided to treat as the equivalent of a loan account, reminds one of this position. On the other hand, where a banker has made demand for repayment of a debit balance and this has not been forthcoming there can be no question of any requirement of notice.

At all events, the very nature of giving notice will generally defeat the banker's objective in that the customer is likely to withdraw the credit balance and leave the debit balance.

The better view is certainly that the accounts can be combined. Many bankers take specific forms of hypothecation; and although if they have done so in particular instances with customers and not done so in other instances with the same customers such a course may operate to the banker's detriment, the basic reason for taking such an authority is to avoid doubt. In other words, such forms merely recapitulate, for the most part, the right that exists.

Turning to the problem, therefore, it is felt that the banker had every right to combine the accounts. The fact that the credit account was a deposit account cannot adversely affect his position. Actually it strengthens the banker's rights and goes towards removing the suggestion that the credit monies should be used for paying cheques. Customarily bankers do not dishonour cheques if they have money on deposit account; but strictly – in the absence of a course dealing to the contrary – the customer has no legal right to draw cheques upon his deposit account.

The question of a banker's charges is one of more contention. In practice the debiting of such charges has not been before the courts, probably because bankers in many instances are unwilling to litigate a relatively small amount and also because customers recognise that services cannot be gratuitous. In fact there has never been a suggestion that they should be. Sometimes it is suggested that by implication interest payable on an overdraft is sufficient profit to a banker. Usually he does not demand more; but in certain instances the trouble associated with conducting an account far transcends any benefit stemming from the payment of interest. In that event charges are justifiable. There appears, however, in *Questions on Banking Practice*, 1963 edition, no. 416, an answer – which although not in any way formally binding would have considerable influence on the establishment of practice and usage – to the effect that a banker is not justified in dishonouring a

116

customer's cheques if he has sufficient funds in his hands to pay them merely because there would be insufficient money due to pay his charges. In other words, the banker may have no right of set-off. Probably this is the true position. Nevertheless in practice – usually because of circumstances – bankers occasionally do debit charges when they anticipate an account is likely to leave them and its history is of an unsatisfactory nature. Whilst this course is justified practically, the strict legal position may be to the contrary. However, in the particular instances outlined in the problem no cheques have been presented and most bankers would debit their charges to the deposit account. As mentioned, their position is the stronger in the particular case case because notice is required in relation to the deposit account.

Thus the banker can with reasonable confidence not only combine the accounts but debit the charges, preferably debiting this sum to the deposit account; this step is certainly more justifiable on the ending of the relationship of banker and customer than would otherwise be the case.

*See also note to Question 2 page 74.

11 : Clearing rules and the customer

Anyfield is a town with five clearing banks who operate a local clearing and Mr X has an account with one of them, namely Lowtown Bank Ltd. To obtain the full benefits of automation, the banks decide to discontinue the clearing and route all items through the London clearing.

Sometime later, Lowtown Bank has a cheque returned to it by one of the local banks which had originally been paid in by Mr X five days previously and which has had a bad answer. Lowtown Bank debits Mr X's account and sends him the cheque by post. The next day Mr X demands to know why there has been such a long delay in his learning of the fate of a 'local' cheque. He complains that he has released goods to the drawer of the cheque and threatens to sue Lowtown Bank because it did not inform him of the new arrangement and because it has not used reasonable care as his agent in securing payment of the cheque and safeguarding his interests.

Discuss the position of Lowtown Bank Ltd.

Before reading the solution it should be borne in mind that it does not emphasise quite sufficiently that the essential point in the case is whether adequate notice of the changed arrangements has been given – expressly or impliedly – to the customer. Without such notice the customer could be entitled to presume that a previously existing system or usage is continued. It should also be kept in mind that in *Burnett* v. *Westminster Bank, Ltd.* (1965 3 All ER 81 (THE BANKERS' MAGAZINE, VOL. CCIII, February 1967, p. 116, vol. cci, April 1966, p. 251, February 1966, p. 116 VOL. CC, August 1965, pp. 92, 93-4, July 1965, pp. 27-8), the judge held that a notice printed on a cheque-book cover was insufficient. (This related to the discontinuance of the ability to use cheques drawn on one branch, if appropriately altered, for an account with another branch.) It is, therefore, a question of fact whether the disappearance of the local clearing had been brought to the notice of the particular customer reasonably – if in fact he can establish that he did not know of the change.

It is natural for Mr X to be upset that he may suffer loss, and unfortunate that he attributes it to the new clearing arrangements of the bank, of which he appears to have been unaware. Usually it is the custom of banks to give adequate and reasonable notice of such new arrangements both in the press and by a notice prominently displayed in full view of the public inside the bank. It is not customary or usual to send individual notices to each customer, nor would it be financially practicable as any customer could always plead that the notice had not been received; so a system of checking acknowledgments would have to be effected. If Mr X himself paid in the cheques it is reasonable to assume that he saw the notice in the bank on previous visits. Even if he did not, as a business man he must have an opportunity of seeing it many times in the local newspaper. He had not asked Lowtown Bank Ltd, to make a special presentment of the cheque and request for its fate, facilities which he would be aware were available to him. As a business man he knew the risk that he took in accepting a cheque; and in these days of lightning strikes he would be unwise to *assume* the cheque was paid when he could have so easily found out definitely. A collecting banker must act strictly in accordance with recognised banking practice, otherwise he may be involved in liability on grounds of negligence. To-day if a cheque is paid in on a Friday morning it is quite possible that it will be the following Friday before the customer can assume it is paid (*i.e.*, 7 days). So it may be suggested that Mr X may have lacked prudence.

Lowtown Bank Ltd could also consider a possible angle of defence of estoppel (*Orbit Mining & Trading Co., Ltd.* v. *Westminster Bank, Ltd.,* 1963). Briefly, this is that a customer may have said or done something which led the collecting bank to believe, on reasonable grounds, that it would be in order for the bank to collect the cheque for his account by the new method.

Scrutton, L.J. in *Greenwood* v. *Martins Bank, Ltd.* (1932), in commenting on the decision in the *Macmillan Case* expressed the important opinion that it establishes a 'continuing duty on either side to act with reasonable care to ensure the proper working of the account'.

We may now examine the position of the banker as a collecting agent pure and simple. As regards the customer for whom he collects cheques, he must act with due care and diligence in presenting the articles for payment. Failure to use the customary and recognised channels may involve him in liability to his customer if the latter suffers loss. In order to obtain the protection of Section 4 of the Cheques Act 1957 the banker must act throughout simply and solely as an agent for his customer.

119

The onus is upon Lowtown Bank, Ltd., to prove that it acted in good faith without negligence. Negligence and failure to act in good faith are distinct: a thing is done in good faith when in fact it is done honestly, whether or not it is done negligently. Lord Wright in *Lloyds Bank* v. *Savory* (1933) opined that a banker does not *inevitably* establish absence of negligence by proving that acts alleged to be negligence are within the ordinary practice of bankers and alleging that a bank is not negligent if it takes all precautions usually taken by bankers. Lord Warrington said however 'The standard by which the absence or otherwise of negligence is to be determined must, in my opinion, be ascertained by reference to the practice of reasonable men carrying on the business of bankers, and endeavouring to do so in such a manner as may be calculated to protect themselves and others against fraud'. The negligence must be negligence in collecting the cheque. In *Forman* v. *Bank of England* (1902) a customer paid in a cheque for £500 drawn on a Norwich bank, alternatively payable in London. The Bank of England passed this cheque through the Country Clearing and dishonoured on the following day a cheque of their customer drawn in reliance on the clearance of the cheque for £500. Evidence was called that it was banking custom to pass cheques so drawn through the Town Clearing and damages were accordingly awarded to the customer. Omission by the collecting banker, Lowtown Bank Ltd, to present and collect local cheques in accordance with the recognised customs governing the local exchange will amount to negligence sufficient to deprive him of the protection which he is afforded by Section 4, but it will, of course, rest upon Mr X, seeking to hold the banker liable, to prove that he had not acted in accordance with recognised practice. The concurrence of the other local banks in abolishing the local clearing amongst them is a factor of great weight in the practice of bankers in favour of Lowtown Bank Ltd.

Throughout its history the London Bankers Clearing House has seen many changes and a stupendous number of cheques pass through it. The use of this clearing is to Mr X's benefit as his bank charges are lower and cheques are normally despatched and paid as expeditiously as possible. It may be to Lowtown Bank Ltd's advantage to examine its books to see if cheques drawn similarly to the one unpaid have previously been presented and unpaid; it would be a useful point in their favour if they were able to stress that Mr X's customer had previously defaulted. It is interesting to note that in *Marfani* v. *Midland Bank Ltd* (1967) Nield, J. stated that the standard of care is

120

to be derived from the ordinary practice of bankers; and the onus lay on the bank to show that it had acted without negligence.

While a banker to whom a cheque is delivered for collection is under a duty to his customer to use reasonable diligence in presenting cheques for payment, the time allowed for presenting a cheque for payment is not laid down by statute. The duty of Lowtown Bank Ltd would depend upon whether it had followed the current usages of bankers and upon the facts of the particular case of this dishonoured cheque. (Sects. 45(2), 74(2), Bills of Exchange Act 1882). Lowtown Bank Ltd is not bound to transmit cheques on the day it receives them; it had until post time the next day for doing so. (*Hare* v. *Henty* 1861, *Royal Bank of Ireland Ltd* v. *O'Rourke* 1962).

In the customer's and its own interests the Lowtown Bank Ltd may well come to an amicable settlement as having endeavoured to safeguard Mr X's interests. It should be advised to explain to Mr X the advantages of special presentation of cheques for which he may require speedy payment. The answer turns upon whether Mr X should have known of the change.

12 : A customer's mental incapacity

*Bill Smith, a widower, and his son, John (his only child) maintain
separate accounts at the Large Bank, Small Village Branch.
The accounts have been satisfactorily conducted over a number
of years. Bill Smith is of advanced years and, after some months
of failing health, is admitted to a nursing home, suffering from
senility. The Large Bank is aware of this, though only through hearsay.*

*A few days later John Smith pays into his own account a cheque
drawn by his father, for the balance of the father's account. He
states that his father has decided to allow him to manage all his
affairs and wishes to transfer the money into his son's name.*

*In view of the known circumstances, is the Large Bank entitled
to question the transaction and can it possibly refuse to pay the cheque?*

*Assuming the Bank paid the cheque, without question, how
would it deal with a subsequent request for cash from Bill Smith?
At this point John Smith had closed his own account and has
already left the district, for an unknown destination, without
informing either his father or the nursing home.*

Although the problem itself may seem complicated, it is virtually
answered by reference to one question that is of daily practical significance to bankers: what evidence does a banker accept as to his customer being *non compos mentis?* The degree of incapacity is usually
regarded as that of being unable to understand the nature of a business
transaction or, more specifically perhaps, unable to understand the
implications of the normal operation of a banking account and of the
drawing of cheques.

The legal position determined by the *Imperial Loan Co.* v. *Stone*
(1892 1 Q.B. 599CA) is that in any contract a person who was *non
compos mentis* is liable to the same extent as someone who was completely sane, except where the lack of mental capacity was known to
the contracting party.

Translating the above principle to that of the relationship between
banker and customer it becomes apparent that the essential aspect is
whether the bank had notice of the mental incapacity.

If there is a *prima facie* indication of the possibility of this being so, as is quite evidently the position obtaining in the circumstances described in the problem, the bank is put on inquiry. Such an inquiry can only be made from a person who is expert, that is to say, from a doctor. If the bank can obtain from the doctor who attends upon the customer a statement that the doctor considers the customer unable to understand the nature of a business transaction, then the account has to be stopped. However, if the doctor indicates that this is not the case or, as is most frequently likely to happen, that he is unable to say, then the banker can continue to operate the account; since if a medical man is unable to give a positive answer it is quite clear that the banker – a layman – cannot be saddled with notice of mental incapacity notwithstanding the quixotic behaviour of his customer. Where the customer is a patient in a home or a hospital then, of course, it is quite easy to put such a question. Where the customer has a doctor who has seen him at all recently then again the answer can usually be obtained. It is sufficient if it is obtained orally and a note made in the Branch records *at the time* the information is received. Where there is no evidence of contact of the customer with a medical man there is admittedly a difficulty; but usually relatives are at least able to arrange for the customer to see a doctor without the customer being aware of the purpose of the meeting.

Where, which is only in exceptional cases, such contact between doctor and customer does not exist and cannot be brought about then references to the Lord Chancellor's Visitors, or perhaps the local Medical Officer of Health may be of assistance; but extreme care should be taken by a banker before approaching any such party. It is far better to arrange for a relative to make such approach.

Although it is mentioned above that the account is stopped, in practice the banker may, with relative safety, allow ordinary routine drawing to be made by a relative, possibly on the strength of that relative's implied or specific indemnity, for a period of some three to six months.

In the case in question, unless John Smith, or presumably in practice his Receiver, can establish that the bank had unambiguous notice of the mental incapacity of Bill Smith, then the short answer is that the bank has no liability having paid away the cash in accordance with the mandate. The approach of senility is by no means precipitate and it would seem unlikely that John Smith or any representative of his will be able to recover the money paid to his son.

Part six : Mortgages

These refer to freehold or leasehold property. Nevertheless it has to be borne in mind that a legal mortgage of a chose in action, that is shares or a debt or a life policy, can be obtained and is very frequently taken by a bank. The essence of a mortgage of a chose in action is that the asset is transferred to the mortgagee upon the understanding that it is re-transferred when the debt is repaid or the other liability that it secures is satisfied. Dealing with land and buildings, the latter being dependent upon the ownership of the land, it is well to remember that there are two types of conveyancing : where title is registered and transfer is, broadly speaking, the entry at the Registry, and unregistered conveyancing where title is effected by the delivery of the deeds with evidence of the history of the title of the transferor. The most important right of the legal mortgagee is to sell. The deposit of deeds with evidence of intention, written or otherwise, will create an equitable mortgage. It is a security, but there is no power of sale. As to the questions :

Question 1
This illustrates the benefit of State secured title.

Question 2
This is the typical problem that will frequently arise.

Question 3
This question involves a problem that arises relatively seldom because of the standing and care of insurance companies.

Question 4
The change in the law and the effect of the new Act (Matrimonial Homes Act 1967) enabling a search to reveal the wife's interest is particularly to be noted. For bankers it is to be observed that the statute covers the position of further advances on current account obviating the need of a further search. The position has been further complicated by the case of *Boland* v *Williams & Glyn's* relating to the trust interest of a party who was in occupation at the time of the charge. The case has been confirmed by the House of Lords.

124

Question 5
The problems relating to second mortgages are more difficult than one would presume from the fact that dispute seldom arises—the question, however, is one of considerable interest.

Question 6
This question, relating to a housing association, is unusual.

Question 7
Forged deeds occur relatively infrequently—there was, however, one instance where the same property was charged to four different banks, there being three sets of forged deeds.

1 : A land certificate obtained by fraud

*In 1964, your customer John Cornhill secured his account with a
second mortgage of 1, Bank Plain, E.C.2, the deeds of which are held
by Lombard Building Society as first mortgagee, under a legal charge
dated 1961. In attempting to enforce your security it is found that, in
1962, by fraudulently declaring that the deeds had been destroyed,
Cornhill obtained a land certificate and immediately sold the property
to an unsuspecting James Poultry.*

*What are your rights and remedies, and what lessons can the
practical banker learn from this?*

The first point to consider is the form of land certificate that will have
been granted to Cornhill. It is probable that it will have been 'possessory' because of Cornhill's inability to produce the deeds, but that
would not necessarily be so. Where deeds have been destroyed, for
example, a statutory declaration is requested, sometimes with the result
that an absolute title is granted by way of first registration. So both of
these contingencies must be considered. Whilst a 'qualified title' may
be given where title is subject to reservations, this is usually subject to
interests arising either before a particular date or subject to the effect
of a particular instrument (see L.R.A. 1925. S.7(1)). Thus this last
mentioned possibility is excluded from the contingencies examined.

The essential quality of a possessory title is that it is subject to the
priorities set out in Section 6 of the Land Registration Act:

Where the registered land is a freehold estate the registration of any
person as first proprietor thereof with a possessory title only shall not
affect or prejudice the enforcement of any estate right or interest adverse
to or in derogation of the title of the first proprietor, and subsisting or
capable of arising at the time of registration of that proprietor; but
save as aforesaid, shall have the same effect as registration of a person
with absolute title.

Again by Section 70(h) such exceptions from registration are 'overriding interests'. Section 71 provides .

When by virtue of any interest or power which is an overriding interest a mortgagee or other person disposes of an estate charge, or right in or upon a registered estate and the disposition is capable of being registered, the registrar shall, if so required, give effect to the disposition on the register.

An example of such a disposition would be the sale by Lombard Building Society if a possessory title only had been granted.

What, it may be asked, is the position of the bank? The section above, describing the effect of possessory title, preserves the position of parties having adverse interests 'subsisting or capable of arising' at the time of the registration. It would not seem that the bank can be brought within this exception because its claim did not subsist, nor, one would think, was it 'capable of arising' at the time of first registration by Cornhill. This latter expression relates to interests that would be subsisting at the time but for contingencies, or which were in executory form. Thus, apart from the possibilities, considered later, there would appear to be no recompense for the bank.

The issue of an absolute title has a different 'effect'. By Section 20 of the Land Registration Act where there is a disposition for value of a freehold estate registered with an absolute title it confers on the transferee 'an estate in fee simple absolute', subject 'to the incumbrances and other entries, if any, appearing on the register'. It is not, however, subject to incumbrances not appearing on the register (apart from overriding interests which do not include mortgages where an absolute freehold title has been granted). Poultry is a transferee for value and can take the freehold free from the claims of the building society, subject to the question of rectification of the register and/or compensation. Similarly, Poultry's title will be free from the mortgage of the bank.

The remaining question is that of rectification and compensation. These possible methods of adjustment are subject to the principle that by Section 20(3) of the Land Registration Act the Register shall not be rectified so as to affect the title of the proprietor in possession, apart from exceptions. The exceptions are when the disposition to him was void, or he has contributed by his own act, neglect or default to the position that has 'arisen'. This is, of course, other than giving effect to overriding interests. By Section 83(1) the indemnity offered by the Crown relates to loss arising from rectification of the register; by subsection (2) it extends to loss suffered where an error or omission has occurred and the register has not been rectified. Clearly the building society will be recompensed, but it is difficult to see how the bank might justify a claim.

Turning to the practical question of the unenviable position in which the bank would appear to find itself, one has to remember that no enquiry could have been made as to the actual possession of the house at the time that the bank took the second mortgage; for, otherwise, the possession of Poultry would have had to have been explained. The existence of an incumbrance is no impediment to registration. This possibility has given rise to the suggestion that any mortgagee (especially in an area of compulsory registration) would be wise to register a caution. However, this a counsel of perfection against the remote contingency. Cornhill has committed criminal offences but that is no comfort to the bank. The absence of deeds will have been the subject of false affidavits but the basic trouble was the omission of the bankers to enquire about the physical occupation at the time of the mortgage.

2 : A share in a house as security

*A is the sole executor of B and, by the terms of the will, is co-beneficiary
equally with C. After payment of debts, the only asset of the estate
is a freehold house, unencumbered by mortgages or charges and
valued at £4,000, the title to which is registered.*

*As the sale of the house is likely to be somewhat protracted,
A wishes to anticipate his share of the estate with a loan from his
bankers.*

*What form should the bank security take against both A's
interest in the estate and the only tangible asset, the house?*

The first question that should occur to the practical banker is whether
the proposition is one within his normal ambit of activities. He is in fact
asked to bridge a gap in point of time and if the customer is of good
reputation he will wish to help, so long as he is reasonably confident
that repayment will be effected within a comparatively short period.
In the latter connection he will wish to be assured that there are no
practical difficulties, such as the need to obtain vacant possession, a
point of particular significance in the light of the Prevention of Evictions
Act* which makes such a problem a little more difficult than it would
otherwise have been. The banker will also want to know whether he is
on risk, for which purpose he will be willing to advance only a proportion, perhaps 70 per cent, of the valuation, unless, of course, the customer's own financial standing is such that he would undoubtedly be able
to meet any deficit. Having decided that he wishes to be secured there
are two courses open to the banker.

He can rely on the half share of the estate due to A and take a mortgage
of the equitable interest.** This can be done by a formal assignment or
by an irrevocable letter addressed to the executor directing payment
to the bank. As the prospective mortgagor is also the sole executor the
former method is preferable although an undertaking could be drafted
to cover the particular position. If the charge of the half share is accepted
the banker must appreciate that he is subject to any unsettled claims
for duty or debts, for which information he will no doubt rely upon a

letter from solicitors acting in the administration of the deceased's estate. If no solicitors are acting, caution obviously has to be exercised because the information is being obtained from A himself. The bank will be in any event ask A to deposit the deeds so that track can be kept of what is happening.

An alternative would be to take a legal mortgage from A *as executor* which would enable the bank to sell in the event of default. However, in this the proceeds would be subject not only to the possible claims of creditors of the estate but also to that of C for a half share of the estate. Therefore only if C joined in the mortgage in respect of his equitable interest would this second course be justifiable since the executor cannot otherwise mortgage the estate property for his personal benefit. If solicitors were acting, notice would be given to them for its practical rather than legal worth. In fact an undertaking from them to pay A's share to the bank in due course is probably what in practice would happen more often than any other course. This would be given with A's authority and his solicitors would control the proceeds.

*The law is now contained in the Protection from Evictions Act 1970

**This view appears to have been approved in Boland v. Williams & Glyn's 1979 A.C. 875 disapproving Cedars Holdings v. Green 1979.

3 : Proceeds of a fire claim as security

*A bank holds an unlimited debenture covering all assets of a
motor dealers' business, and the account at the bank is substantially
overdrawn. The bank has already given notice in the usual manner
to an insurance company of its interest.*

*The customer pays in an insurance company's cheque, payable
jointly to the bank and the customer, for fire damage to a vehicle.
The bank is aware that the vehicle in question is subject to hire
purchase. On the same day that the bank receives the cheque, it also
receives a letter from the hire purchase company demanding
that the cheque be endorsed by the bank and passed over to them.
The bank hire purchase company points out that the bank has no right
to the insurance money as the damaged vehicle did not belong to the
motor dealer. There has been no question of release from the debenture
given by the bank at any time.*

Was the bank correct in crediting the cheque to the customer's account?

There are three subjects involved in this question: the nature of a
floating charge, the right to insurance monies, and the implications of
a hire purchase agreement.

The question states that a bank holds an unlimited debenture covering all the assets of a motor dealer. Because these assets are not fixed
it is clear that a floating charge is contained in the debenture and that
the borrowing customer is, of course, a limited company. A floating
charge, as with any other security, covers contingencies and when one
of the contingencies arises the bank has a right to exercise its dominion
over the assets, which is done by the appointment of a receiver. Alternatively, if a liquidator takes control of the assets he must recognise the
appropriate priority of the bank. The contingency with a bank debenture
is repayment on demand and until that time the company is authorised
to continue business in the ordinary course. If it carries out transactions
outside the ordinary course it will be in breach. However, the realisation
of one vehicle as a result of a fire is hardly a transaction outside the
ordinary run of business, in that it is not engineered by the company.
Therefore, *prima facie,* unless the bank has made demand the company

is entitled to the proceeds of any assets it owns.

As to insurance monies, these represent the proceeds of an indemnity contract between the company and the insurers. Where notice of any assignment of these monies is received then the party paying under the contract will ensure that the assignee – the bank in the present instance (and possibly in other instances the HP company if it has given notice) – would be asked to give the insurers a discharge, usually jointly with the insured for avoidance of doubt.

A hire purchase agreement is fundamentally a contract of hire with an option to purchase for the hirer when a certain number of hire payments have been made. The vehicle belongs to the hire purchase company (in which case agreement implicitly or explicitly is likely to contain provisions covering the possibility of fire). The surplus or equity in any particular hire purchase contract, which may be for one or more vehicles, is caught by the floating charge only if it has become fixed.

In the problem we are told that the floating charge has not become fixed and therefore the bank itself has no claims to the monies. The point is that it has been requested to collect the cheque payable to the company customer jointly with itself (because notice has been given and the insurers do not know that the charge has not become fixed). The further aspect is whether in the circumstances the bank should collect the cheque because of the claims from the hire purchase company and the risk of conversion. To do so without enquiry would risk the loss since as joint payee the bank has a responsibility. The rights of hire purchase companies are probably paramount because the agreement will have so provided in the event of fire. At all events the bank must enquire, unless the amount is so small compared with the financial standing of the company customer that it is confident that the account will always stand the amount of the claim, in which event the customer could be left to settle the matter with the hire purchase company direct. Otherwise the bank is on enquiry as to what part, if any, of the cheque belongs to its customer. If the cheque had been payable to the company alone the position would have been different, but where the bank is a joint payee the risk of liability cannot be eliminated if the money is made available unconditionally to the company.

4 : The wife's title to mortgaged property

Your customer, A, has secured his overdraft by the legal mortgage of the house in which he and his wife live. The account becomes dormant and you make demand on A who, it transpires, has disappeared. On attempting to exercise your power of sale you are informed by Mrs A that prior to your legal mortgage the deeds were conveyed in her name, and she produces the conveyance as evidence. She resists the sale. What are your rights and remedies?

It is quite clear that the problem of the bank in this instance is going to be to establish the evidence as to what happened. First, it is apparent that if the wife has in any way been involved in connivance at her husband's fraud then she cannot benefit. Against this there is the latitude with which the courts are prepared to treat a married woman who enters into a legal transaction with her husband. If she has not benefited gratuitously but has paid him for the property – and can prove that this is so – then she is most likely to be able to succeed in that the legal estate that belonged to her husband has been transferred to her.

The question is however by no means as simple as that. The law is unwilling that a person who has been grossly negligent shall benefit as a consequence. The legal position of a purchaser is epitomised in Cheshire's *Law of Real Property* Edn 6th at page 64 which merits quotation :

The conveyancing practice of this country demands that a person who is buying land should examine the vendor's deeds in order both to ascertain whether a good title can be made and to ensure that no third person possesses rights which can be enforced against the land. It follows from this that, if a purchaser deliberately omits to call for the title deeds, and allows them to remain in the possession of a third person, he will be deemed to have notice of any equitable claims which the possessor of the deeds may have against the land.

One or two cases may illustrate this principle although it must be appreciated that the actual result will depend upon particular circumstances. In an old case (*Roberts* v. *Croft,* 1857 24 Beav. 223) a solicitor made an equitable deposit of title deeds with a client omitting the conveyance to himself which he deposited with his bank as security. The client was given priority. Again, in the case of *Oliver* v. *Hinton* (1899 Ch. 264), the owner deposited deeds as a security with a lender, and some two years later sold the property. The purchaser enquired about the deeds and was told that they related also to another property and were being retained, but did nothing about examining them. It was held that he was postponed to the mortgagee. He was innocent but negligent and suffered in consequence. Again in *Northern Counties of England Fire Insurance Co. Ltd.* v. *Whipp* (1884 26 Ch. D. 482), the company's manager mortgaged his property to the company and handed over the deeds. Later he obtained the deeds, suppressed the mortgage to the company, and mortgaged them elsewhere. It was held that the company had priority. Mere carelessness about custody of the deeds was distinguished from the failure to call for them at the time of a mortgage or, of course, a purchase.

Thus we see that the position of the bank will depend on the facts. If the transfer or sale to the wife took place in the ordinary way with the assistance of a solicitor acting for the wife and the husband stole the deeds then the bank is without remedy if the wife did not connive at the theft – which would be almost impossible to prove. In contrast to connivance or fraud involving the wife, it is difficult to see any basis upon which the bank could set up a valid claim to be a mortgagee. The title in the property has become vested in the wife and the attempt by the husband to create a mortgage is of no effect. It may perhaps be suggested that as between parties other than close relatives deeds should be kept under lock and key and that the consequences of negligence – to which further reference is made below – have to be considered. However, no one could put forward a suggestion that a wife should keep deeds of property she owns out of reach of her husband, unless, remotely, he had previously stolen property belonging to her.

Where a purchaser fails to call for the deeds, other than the immediate conveyance, this, as has been noted, is *prima facie* evidence of negligence and the purchaser may find himself estopped from claiming that the third party could not set up title to the property. This would be possible even as between husband wife. The legal position is that if a reasonable and acceptable explanation is offered then there is no negligence. It is not enough to be told that the deeds relate to other property. This must be verified. There may however be other excuses that it is reasonable to accept. The relationship of husband and wife would be conducive to this being established. A wife would not necessarily be expected to use a solicitor when acquiring property from her husband, although even then in certain cases such failure to obtain advice may be regarded as negligence.

The problem in practice then turns on the extent to which the bank can obtain evidence as to what happened – the questions to ask the wife are whether she received advice, whether she paid any money and under what circumstances she acquired the property. She may in fact be unaware of the transaction and in law may be no more than her husband's nominee. One likely possibility is the bankruptcy of the husband – if thought worthwhile. He is indebted to the bank, which obligation he must repay or in the long run be subject to bankruptcy.

Then if no consideration had been paid by the wife the conveyance could be upset within two years irrespective of whether the husband was solvent at the time of the conveyance. Whether consideration passed is always difficult to establish between husband and wife, since monies may be intermixed and the conveyance will have recited a consideration. The price of property is, nevertheless, relatively large. The task of the bank in obtaining evidence is however very difficult and control and investigation of the husband's affairs through a trustee in bankruptcy may be the best way of ascertaining the facts.

Quite apart from title it is open to the wife to register, by way of precautions, a Land Charge F as soon as she learns of a competing claim. This will protect her possessory right against any future mortgagee if her husband eventuates to be the owner.

5 : Notice of second mortgage

*Mr X, a director, deposits the deeds of his house valued at £3,500
as security for a company's account at Old Bank. The company's
overdraft is £10,000 and other directors deposit security valued
at £8,000; there is also a joint and several guarantee for £10,000.
Mr X conducts his private account at New Bank and gives them
a second mortgage on his house. New Bank gives notice to
Old Bank of the second mortgage. What figure does Old Bank
give as reply to the question of amount owing on the charge in
their favour?*

The first practical aspect occurring to a banker is why New Bank did
not ascertain how much was owing under the Old Bank mortgage
before actually taking the second mortgage. Possibly it was taken on an
oral assurance from Mr X as to how much was thought to be the
liability to the Old Bank; or perhaps New Bank have taken the mortgage but have not lent any money. One would expect the position still
to be flexible at the time of the enquiry – this would very much ease
the practical solution to which reference is made later.

The legal position is that normally a bank mortgage is for all monies
owing by the customer and therefore, although there is other security
held, Old Bank may resort to the deeds of Mr X for the whole of the
indebtedness of the company for whose account it is charged as security.
It is to be noted that there is a joint and several guarantee of the
directors, each of whom has charged security, so that this other security
is available proportionately as between the directors personally. This,
of course, does not affect the right of the bank to regard each item of
security as available for the maximum overdraft of the company,
whether or not it is more than £10,000. The deeds have been charged
on a separate mortgage for the company's borrowing and the mortgage
is not limited to the amount of the guarantee liability. As mentioned,
more obviously even, it is not limited to the relative proportion of all the
security deposited by the directors. The answer to the New Bank is
that the amount owing on first mortgage is the amount owing by the
company (with interest) at the date such notice is received. The com-

pany's account will be stopped in the usual way to avoid the operation of the Rule in Clayton's Case (*Devaynes* v. *Noble*, 1816 1 AER 529), and the decision in *Deeley* v. *Lloyds Bank* (1912 A.C. 756) AER. Other security, which is also not charged specifically in support of the guarantee, will still be available and it is likely that Old Bank will open a new account and permit an overdraft, probably approximately equivalent to any balance of the facility.

There are several practical solutions. Perhaps the most simple would be if Old Bank is willing to limit the extent to which it looks to the deeds of Mr X as cover. We are told that the other directors have deposited security worth £8,000. Thus in broad terms, as the Bank has security of £11,500 to secure an overdraft of £10,000, it may be prepared to limit its claim against the deeds to £3,000. This £500 equity may be sufficient for the facility at New Bank. If, however, some of the £8,000 security consists of quoted shares Old Bank may be unwilling to take the risk of the £8,000 valuation diminishing. Another possible solution may be that the company will require a smaller facility in the future, thus permitting a measure of reduction in the extent to which Old Bank wishes to look to the deeds of Mr X. It is even possible that other security will be available permitting the deeds to be released altogether, although this is unlikely to be acceptable to the other directors. Whatever is decided, it is open to Old Bank to agree by endorsement of the mortgage that it is not to be security for more than a specific maximum amount. In practice there is likely to be a meeting between Old Bank, Mr X and other representatives of the company, at which a solution is likely to be found. On the face of the matter Old Bank is entitled to talk to the company about the limitation on the security, although not to New Bank – without appropriate authority from the company and Mr X.

(An interesting side issue is whether if the balance was £10,000 at Old Bank, and New Bank had already lent the money, New Bank would have been able completely to step into the shoes of Mr X and obtain his right of contribution against the other depositors of security (and reimbursement from the company) if Mr X's deeds were sold, perhaps by Old Bank as mortgagees, and applied in reduction of the indebtedness. The better view is that New Bank would succeed to such rights of Mr X.)

6 : Undertaking from a housing association

*A customer selling his house mortgaged to a building society
under a life endowment policy scheme requires the life policy to
arrange a new mortgage on the house he is buying. He asks the bank
to pay off the mortgage pending the receipt of the sale proceeds.
The bank agrees subject to the normal solicitor's undertaking, etc.
They receive instead a letter from a housing association which
is acting on the customer's behalf in which an undertaking is
offered. Should the bank accept this and if so what risk does it take?*

When bankers accept a solicitor's undertaking they usually have in
view their own claims for which it is to be cover. In fact there is however another aspect that has to be borne in mind, that they are acting
on their customer's instruction. Often deeds will be sent to a solicitor
and a banker protects himself by obtaining a solicitor's undertaking.
In delivering the deeds to a solicitor he is acting as his customer's
agent. If he parts with deeds to any particular party he must have his
customer's instructions. These instructions must be precise. Thus, if
an undertaking is offered from a source different from that intimated
by the customer, it is prudent to ensure that such course accords with
the customer's intentions. It may be thought to be obvious that the
undertaking will be offered only by someone acting in pursuance to
the customer's instructions – but, although highly probable, this does
not follow inevitably where a transaction is at all complex and there
are a number of parties involved.

Before adverting to the specific question it is worth mentioning that
the clearing banks have agreed with the Law Society a number of
standard forms for general use. Occasionally it may be necessary for
these forms to be adapted and it follows that this should be done only
with the maximum care, as involving either professional guidance or
head office authority, according to the rules of the particular bank
concerned. In parenthesis, there is one other point to bear in mind.
Bankers will be aware that solicitors' undertakings are invariably
honoured; if there is a rare exception this is likely to be remedied from
a central source. In one instance only is special thought necessary.

Where a company is involved and the banker has not already had the deeds charged to him *and thus not registered in the Companies Register,* there is the possibility that, even after the solicitor has honoured his undertaking by the delivering of the deeds to the banker (possibly as an alternative way of fulfilling his obligation), there may be no true security. A mortgage by a company with or without possession of the deeds is void against a creditor or liquidator if not registered at the Companies Registry, although it is good against the company itself. This may mean in an exceptional instance that a banker has become a mortgagee, probably by actual or constructive possession of the deeds, but that his charge is bad against the liquidator to whom he must deliver them. The remedy, again to be followed in most institutions only after reference to head office, may be to register the undertaking against the company, either as an equitable charge or as the deposit of deeds (held of course by the solicitor as agent); this may necessitate the under-taking being given *on behalf of the* company but solicitors will probably appreciate the problem. *It is to be emphasised however that in practice this aspect is likely to be relevant only if the banker is hesitant about the financial standing of the company or very large amounts are involved. Even then the point is one of which it is worth being aware only in order to seek guidance.*

There is then the question of the bank's security. It has been custo-mary to rely upon the undertakings of solicitors because they are men of integrity. Also the possession by them of the deeds has always been necessary for sale or purchase; incidentally they frequently report whether the title is good and marketable. If however deeds – or any other security – had to be left with a chartered accountant, for example, his undertaking would no doubt be regarded as quite satisfactory. Solicitors' undertakings are given regularly and operate to the satis-faction of all concerned. They are from men of integrity. It is possible that a banker might be hesitant to rely upon an undertaking from a particular person but be quite prepared to accept the assurance of some third party. The competence of the party concerned and the efficacy of the work done is normally not a matter for concern. It is for the banker to get an independent report if he wishes.

There are of course housing associations that are covered by the Housing Acts and operate under the indirect aegis of the Minister acquiring, for example, houses to let. Any other group or association will be dependent upon its standing as to the worth of the undertaking, but, if the bank is hesitant about the validity of title then, whoever the party concerned may be, it is for him to be separately professionally advised.

Thus – a banker follows his customer's instructions if he is not concerned with the item as a security; in the latter event he will be dependent on the standing of the party from whom an undertaking is forthcoming. As to the quality of advice received, as with a report or title that he finds unacceptable, it is open to him and desirable to get independent guidance.

7 : Forged deeds

Mr X, a customer of long standing, approaches the manager of Large Town branch to lend him £50,000 against the security of freehold deeds professionally valued at £75,000, and which the branch have held informally in their security register for the past two years and are satisfied as to title and fire cover. The bank's head office agree, on being informed, that the source of repayment is to be an insurance company loan against paid up policies within four months. This is confirmed. The money is supposedly to be used to float a new company.

Just before repayment is due the branch is advised of the existence of a receiving order, which is later confirmed. Furthermore it transpires that the customer has forged a duplicate set of the deeds which have deceived a solicitor acting for a client who has advanced £35,000 against the deeds and who holds a legal mortgage.

What is the bank's position as equitable mortgagee and would the position be different if both the mortgagees had only equitable charges?

It will be seen as the various aspects of the problem are examined that there are certain alternative possibilities as to the facts, but recognition of these is part of the solution, the question having been left in precisely the wording in which it was submitted. There are a number of different subjects involved; in each case there is the general legal position to be noted, which then has to be applied to the facts of the case. There are four subjects to be considered : the creation of the equitable mortgage; the rights against the policies; the claims of the holders of the forged deeds; and the position of the trustee in bankruptcy.

The first point that will be observed is that the deeds were recorded in the *security* register. Branch bookkeeping methods differ but many offices have a 'safe custody' register, which would have been an indication, if the deeds had been recorded in it, that they were specifically excluded from the category of security in the absence of further evidence. In fact where share certificates (*Re United Service Co.* 1870 6 Ch. App. 212) or probably life policies (*Re Bowes* 1886 33 Ch. D. 586) are so held, the banker has a lien involving a power of sale over such items. With securities closer in character to negotiable instruments, such as deposit receipts or orders for payment, the principle is applied with even less difficulty, but with deeds it is thought that the banker's lien, being limited to securities in a more restricted definition than as now regarded in a branch bank, is ineffective. This does not mean that the banker cannot become an equitable mortgagee but only that he cannot automatically retain the deeds in respect of any liability of the customer. An equitable mortgage can be created without writing – this was decided as long ago as 1873 in *Russell* v. *Russell* (1783 2 W. & T.L.C. 76). For example, if at the time of the original deposit the customer has said (and evidence of this could now be produced) 'these will be available if I should ever borrow from you' it would probably be sufficient. What is more probable – or in fact is stated in the question – is that the customer asked the bank to lend him money 'against the security of the deeds'. This, which can be evidenced no doubt by a bank official and which is probably contained in current branch reports of the matter to its head office, will be sufficient to establish the bank as an equitable mortgagee from the time that the intention was evidenced by the customer and the bank was committed to lend if the latter time was after the intention was made known.

The rights against the policies is the least difficult question. From what we are told there appears to have been no suggestion that they were the bank's security. It is not clear whether the policies (which were paid-up policies) were in existence. It is however almost certain that they were either not in existence or not available (perhaps charged elsewhere) as security, because an insurance company will normally lend quickly against such policies, which would have avoided the need for bank borrowing. There may have been at some time before the fraudulent revelations an instruction to pay the bank in the hands of an insurance company. An irrevocable authority is certainly an equitable assignment and there has been a case in which a simple instruction given for a consideration has been held to give the person to whom it is addressed a right to the benefit of the monies concerned (*Bell* v. *L.N.W. Rly. Co.* (1852 15 Beav. 548)), approved in the judgment in *Re Kent & Sussex Sawmills* (1947 Ch. 177). This is obviously only an incidental aspect, but is a practical although unlikely possibility in the case under examination.

The claims of the holder of the forged deeds are the crux of the problem. It must be remembered that the title to the property was at all

142

material times vested in Mr X. He was the true owner. The possession of deeds or of forged deeds by a mortgagee or a purchaser does not mean that a mortgage or conveyance *by the person in whom the title was vested* is bad. There is often, however, a competition between two or more claimants. The possession of forged deeds may lead an innocent party to presume that there he has first claim as mortgagee or that he is the transferee in the event of a sale. Registered title to property is, of course, excluded from this discussion but the rights of the parties may be affected by registration of charges. The person who has the duplicate deeds has a legal mortgage. He is not, on the other hand, a mortgagee with the deeds, he is the holder of a puisne mortgage – that is to say a legal mortgagee unprotected by possession of the deeds. As such his position is vulnerable against two parties: a mortgagee with the deeds, whether that mortgage is legal or equitable, and against any other puisne mortgagee who has registered his mortgage earlier in point of time. Thus if in the question, as may be presumed, the bank was the earlier mortgagee, it has a good title. If by chance the duplicate deeds were deposited and the mortgage for £35,000 given to the solicitors' client before the date on which the bank became equitable mortgagee, then if, and *only if,* that client had had his earlier mortgage registered as a puisne mortgage (that is a Land Charge C (i)), *and* the bank had not searched when becoming equitable mortgagees, would the bank have lost its priority. This is almost out of the question because no one in possession of deeds registers as a puisne mortgagee, unless perhaps he thinks there is a missing deed, and a banker invariably searches before, and usually just after, he lends money against deeds. It is appropriate to consider at this juncture the position if the mortgagee with the false deeds had held only an equitable mortgage. It is difficult to see how this could have affected matters except that the registration would have been as a general equitable charge (C (iii)). Its appearance on the register would have had a similar effect on the bank as if a puisne mortgage had been registered.

There remains the position of the trustee in bankruptcy. The sequence in bankruptcy of the material events is: act of bankruptcy; a petition; a receiving order and subsequently, adjudication. A bankruptcy petition may be registered as a Pending Action at the Land Charges Registry (Land Charges Act s. 2(1)). Similarly a receiving order is registrable in the Register of Writs and Orders Affecting Land (Land Charges Act ss. 6 & 7). If the petition is unregistered a purchaser or mortgagee is still bound by it unless he acquires the legal estate and has no notice of an act of bankruptcy. The position is the same with a receiving order. Thus, if there had been failure to register a bankruptcy entry prior to either of the mortgages, only a legal mortgagee could in any event have gained advantage from such absence of registration. However, such registration is virtually automatic in the case of receiving orders and is hardly relevant. Certainly the implication in the question is that the receiving order was made near to the time when repayment was almost due. If it is subsequent to the bank mortgage then it has no effect, come what may, on money lent four months before. Also any relevant act of bankruptcy and petition must have been within the preceding three months and therefore after bank became a mortgagee.

Part seven : Miscellaneous securities

There is no end to the type of security. Where there is an asset, such even as an interest in an estate of a deceased person, a security can be given to the bank. Often an irrevocable authority to a third party to pay money is taken, which in law is an equitable assignment and in practice is effective.

As to the questions :

Question 1
A postponement is a very useful right to a lender. In essence it is a charge or at least has the same effect as illustrated in the question.

Question 2
This question savours of banking policy perhaps more than law—it is seldom that disputes arise.

Question 3
This deals with the very important subject of a lien. Bankers have a right of sale where they have a lien although the ability to make title does not follow without great assistance, unless the item concerned, such as a bill of exchange or a bearer share is concerned is fully negotiable.

Question 4
Normally the bank will look to the proceeds of a fire policy, but will not mind it being expended on rebuilding. Where, however, a leaseholder also is involved, negotiations are in practice quite protracted. The answer will be quite helpful to those concerned.

Question 5
This is really practical banking. Probably there is no lack of good faith, but the contrary contingency has to be borne in mind.

K

1 : Implications of a loan postponement

The security for a company's overdraft consists of a Loan Postponement Form signed by loan creditors confirming that they will not, without the consent of the bank, withdraw their loan funds, and countersigned on behalf of the company to the effect that it will not repay these funds without the consent of the bank.

The bank, being concerned about the company's financial position, is endeavouring, unsuccessfully, to obtain reductions in the borrowing and after requesting sight of the latest and recently produced audited accounts is surprised to observe that the loan moneys have been repaid during the financial period.

What should the bank do in these circumstances and what are its legal rights against (a) the company; and (b) the loan creditors?

The taking by bankers of loan postponement forms is a fairly frequent step in some banks. Although, as was mentioned in nearly all the answers, the completion of such an undertaking is not normally regarded as a security, its attraction stems from the banker's interest in the customer's balance sheet. If this indicates loans of any substantial amount from directors or other private persons a banker visualises these as competing creditors in any liquidation and their repayment as a possible source of depletion of the available liquid assets at a future time, with consequent embarrassment for the customer's trading.

The idea of ensuring that this finance shall not be peremptorily withdrawn is natural. It may even be that the loans represent an accumulation of claims by the individuals against the customer or perhaps part of a generous price paid when the business was sold by the former owners to a limited company. It was emphasised in the answers that primarily a form of postponement, to which detailed reference is made below, is a contractual obligation. Even less perhaps, many bankers may regard it as little more than a deterrent. It often, however, turns out to have stronger implications.

Of necessity, and desirably in order to give the question a reasonably wide scope, no particular wording was mentioned in the question. The form, of course, in practice varies from bank to bank, and some banks may have more than one type in use. The question indicated, however, that the form not only contained an undertaking by the creditor not to withdraw without consent of the banker but also was countersigned by the company complementarily. Thus quite clearly both the creditor and the company would be in breach if some of the moneys were withdrawn without the consent of the banker, if in fact a facility was still being provided. The form may in some instances in addition give to the banker a right to receive any dividend paid on the loan moneys in the event of liquidation.

From a legal standpoint the character of the postponement may well depend on its terms. That it falls short of an assignment by way of security was emphasised by a number of correspondents. Certainly an attempt to enforce its terms as if it were an assignment would encounter practical difficulties. Whether in fact such an attempt would ultimately fail is not so certain. To take perhaps an extreme view one may look at the nature of a postponement and appreciate that, so far as concerns the postponer, that person cannot enjoy the benefit of the asset (that is, the loan) until the banker has been repaid. In one sense such an arrangement comes very close to being a charge, in that there is a restriction upon the enjoyment, realisation or other disposition of the asset without either the concurrence of the party in whose favour the form of postponement has been completed or, as with other securities generally, the repayment of the indebtedness of the customer to the banker.

For the purpose of this answer sufficient indication has been given of the possible strength of the simple postponement. Whether or not it amounts to an equitable charge does not ever appear to have come before the courts and is, of course, open to the contention that its wording does not amount, specifically, to an assignment, which the parties could have stated in clear terms had they wished. On the other hand, it needs, as between debtor and creditor, very little in law to achieve an equitable assignment and perhaps the balance of possibilities is that one day a postponement of its nature may be held by the courts to amount to a charge on the debt concerned. All the more is this likely to be the case if the form of postponement enables the banker to claim the dividend in lieu of the loan holder in the event of liquidation (involving in the case of a limited company postponing, registration under Section 95 of the Act). In this latter connection it is of interest that the banker holding such a form may prevent a loan holder from voting at a meeting of creditors, thus permitting trade creditors, who might otherwise be outvoted by private loan holders, to determine the issues put to the meeting. In some circumstances many people might regard that as commercially and morally desirable. Signature by the company of the form will, of course, ensure that notice has been received by the loan debtor, which is an essential of any assignment of a loan. It should in practice prevent such repayment which could take place if the company did not know.

There is quite a choice for the banker in practice. That there are breaches of contract stands out. This means that he could sue the recipient to recover the amount paid or the amount of the indebtedness of the customer, whichever is the greater. This may or may not be a satisfactory remedy. A contingently even more fragile course would be to sue the company : this appears to be largely academic because the company is always liable to the banker on demand and could be sued direct. In the event of liquidation of the company the banker is probably entitled to receive a dividend instead of the loan holder and is certainly so entitled if the form of postponement specifically says so, which is often the case. However, liquidation may not appeal to the banker, although unfortunately it may be brought about by the initiative of others. In the event of liquidation the repayment of loans might be attacked as fraudulent (*i.e.,* voidable) preferences, but evidence of pressure from the loan holder may well eliminate such claim, which certainly is not so strong *vis à vis* the party repaid as a separate action for breach of the contractual obligation. On the other hand it may possibly permit third parties involved in the repayment to be assailed.

It is perhaps appropriate to add that the view might be taken that if A postpones a loan from C Ltd in favour of B, he is in fact postponing his claim to every other creditor who stands in the same position as B, but it is thought that there is no substantiation for this point of view.*

* It has found some support, however, in New Zealand in Re Walker Construction Co. Ltd. (1960 N.Z.L.R. 523)

2 : Children and National Savings Certificates

A customer informs his manager that he is buying a house and part of the purchase price is to be provided by the encashment of National Savings Certificates in the names of his two children aged 8 and 17, for approximately £150 and £350 respectively. The bank is asked to prepare the forms for signature and in due course to credit the repayment warrants to the father's account. What risks exist for the bank? What suggestions can be made to help the father?

National Savings Certificates are occasionally taken as a bank security although a legal mortgage cannot be obtained. An equitable charge is created by the deposit of the certificates, which are accompanied by a repayment form signed by the holder. Disadvantages are the risk of duplicate certificates being obtained and the fact that the Director of Savings declines to accept notice. The problem in this case does not, of course, concerned the mortgaging of certificates. The bank, however, is made aware of the interest of the children in the certificates and whether the warrants are payable to them or to the father is not material from the standpoint of the bank. The point at issue is that the bank is aware of the way in which the certificates were held. Presuming, for the present, that there is no possibility that the customer can give any explanation by which he is beneficially entitled, the banker is faced with the question of trusteeship. So long as the customer cannot establish that his children had no interest in the certificates then the banker is saddled with the notice of trust. He is aware that the funds belong to the children. If he makes the money available to the father, it is possible, although from a practical aspect unlikely, that at some later date there will be a claim on behalf of the children. Such an event could arise if there were a dispute or divorce between husband and wife. The wife would know of the children's interest and, being in touch with solicitors in relation to matrimonial proceedings, would be likely to refer to the matter. If the husband had no money with which to reimburse the children a claim against the bank is feasible. For this reason there is a risk

– admittedly limited in amount – if it became involved in their customer's request. If the husband were of undoubted means the bank would be insulated from that risk because it would look to him by way of indemnity, but if he were of a financial standing far beyond the figures involved, the problem would not arise at all.

What advice can be given to the husband? The first thought is that a trust could be created. Trustees can generally lend against a first mortgage and then only up to two-thirds of the value of the property. To set up a trust with powers to do otherwise would be tantamount to depriving the children. It needs only a little thought to appreciate that a trust with, for example, power to lend to an impecunious father is of no advantage to the children. One has to realise that there can be no presumption that property values will not fall during the period of the trust, despite current economic theories and their probable long-term effect on the value of money. A second course would be to establish a trust for the children of the property (which they would own at 21), the parents paying rent which would repay any building society mortgage. This would be unassailable but would probably have no appeal to the parents. To give the parents a life interest in the property may not do justice to the children and perhaps would require, and not receive, sanction of the court. Such a trust could be established, however, giving the parents a right within a particular period to pay the children an amount equivalent to the money provided and accumulated interest, against release of their interest in the house.

All the foregoing is complicated in the light of the amounts involved. It has been presumed that the cash in question would form the bulk of the deposit on a house purchase. Obviously if the father had other assets or himself was contributing a relatively large amount the position of the children could be secured. In any event, the bank would decide either to take the risk or insist on paying the monies to trustees for the benefit of the children. The above problem would be involved in the creation and administration of that trust. The Savings Certificates may be in the name of the children absolutely and not in the name of the father as trustee, but the difficulty of gifts from minors to their parents (where the parents are not to be trustees) creates very much a similar problem for the banker encashing the certificates. It may perhaps be said that the child of 17 and not the child of 8 can give the money to the parent, since the elder child has a mental capacity to appreciate what is involved but the point is open to doubt.

150

3 : A banker's lien
and a joint and several liability

Mr A has a current account and Mr and Mrs A have a joint account at the Northtown Bank. Both accounts are credit accounts. Mr A has left with the bank his deeds worth £5,000 and £1,000 of War Stock worth say, £600. Mr and Mrs A, who are of good reputation, go abroad. Two cheques are presented, the one for £600 drawn by Mr A on his own account and the other for £400 drawn by Mrs A on the joint account. Expecting a letter from the customers at a later date, the manager pays the cheques. Both Mr and Mrs A are killed in an air crash and the only assets of size belonging to either are the deeds and the War Stock. They owe some £7,000 to a number of other creditors. What is the position of the bank?

It is implicit in the question that the cheques overdrew the accounts. Obviously the creditors' claims are greater than the assets available; the problem is whether the bank has a right to be repaid in full from the proceeds of the War Stock and, if necessary, the deeds, or whether either or both of these items has to be made available for the unsecured creditors.

The first point to be noted is that the War Stock and the deeds belong to the husband. A banker's lien will arise in respect only of liabilities of the owner of the securities in respect of which a lien is claimed. Clearly any lien that exists relates to the liabilities of the husband. He is liable on his own account and also on the joint account. This liability on a joint account is in practice almost always made into a joint and several liability by the undertaking contained in the mandate completed by customers opening such an account. Such provision avoids many difficulties, including those involved in the death or bankruptcy of one of the account holders.

Whilst there is no reason why a banker's lien should not apply in respect of a liability where the owner of the asset is only jointly liable to the banker, it is highly probable that the liability will in fact be joint and several. Thus, in so far as a lien is available to the banker, it will be good for the borrowing on the joint account as well as on the husband's own account.

A banker's lien is different from a general lien. Strictly a lien is a right of a creditor to retain what he holds belonging to the debtor. It does not permit the creditor to sell the asset as does a banker's lien, which has been described as an implied pledge (*Brandao* v. *Barnett* 1846 12 Cl. & Fin. 787) – a pledgee, of course, having a right to sell as soon as the remedy is available. This lien is excluded by evidence of a contrary intention; for example, if the item has been deposited specifically in safe custody or for a particular purpose only, such as providing cover up to a limited figure, the right of the banker to retain the securities does not arise. Again, if the item is known to belong to the holder as a trustee, the lien, being in a different right, does not arise. It appears, therefore, that in the case under consideration the banker's lien has not been excluded and can be utilised in respect of either the husband's account or the joint account.

The further question is as to what property is covered by the lien. In the case mentioned above, *Brandao* v. *Barnett,* it was stated to extend to all securities coming into the hands of the banker in the course of his business as a banker. In an earlier case *Davis* v. *Bowsher* (1794. 5. Terms Rep. 488) the expression 'all paper securities' was used. It has been held to apply to share certificates (*Re* United Service Co. 1870 6 Ch. App. 212) and, as one would expect, not only to cheques and fully negotiable instruments but to deposit receipts and orders to pay falling outside the definition of a cheque. From the case of *Re* Bowes (*Strathmore* v. *Vane*) 1886, 33 Ch. D. 586 there is an implication that it is applicable to a life policy. There is, however, a decision indicating that it is not applicable to deeds. In the case of *Wylde* v. *Radford* (1863. 33 L.J. Ch. 51) a customer deposited a conveyance relating to two properties with his bankers, giving a charge over one of the properties. It was held that the bankers had no lien upon the document in respect of the other property. It may be suggested that the circumstances of the deposit may amount to the specific exclusion of a lien on the second property and that it was that fact, and not the nature of the security, that prevented the lien arising. The remarks of the Vice-Chancellor in the case unfortunately indicate that the reason for the decision was that the lien did not go beyond a more limited category.

Reverting to the problem, therefore, the bank would find difficulty in claiming reimbursement from the proceeds of the deeds, although the War Stock could be retained and sold. The proceeds could be used to repay the debit balance on the husband's account or on the joint account. There may of course in practice be sufficient evidence to

152

indicate an intention on the part of the husband that the deeds were to be security for his liabilities; a mention of the matter at any time would be sufficient.

There is one other aspect that would be relevant only if the liability were joint and not joint and several. The parties were killed in an air crash. The elder would be presumed to have died first in the absence of contrary evidence. If the husband had been the elder, it may have been contended successfully that the liability became that of the wife alone on the husband's death and that there was no claim against *him*. This contingency would not apply where there was a joint and several responsibility of the parties.

4 : The proceeds of a fire policy

Mr A has deposited with XYZ Bank Limited the deeds of his house to cover his banking account. Included is the fire insurance policy, and in accordance with the usual practice the bank has given notice of its interest in the property to the insurance company and has received an acknowledgement. The bank now finds that some time ago the property was destroyed by fire and that the insurance company has paid over the claim monies to Mr A.
What is the position of the bank?

It is perhaps more easy to deal first with the practical aspects. Security is from a banking aspect, theoretically at all events, secondary to the integrity of the customer. If the customer is a person of integrity the bank will possibly be willing for a house to be rebuilt and there is no indication in the question that the customer has not used the money for the purpose of restoring the house. This would be particularly the case if it was the residence of a customer. If on the other hand the monies have been utilised by the borrower for some other purpose, then the banker will wish to pursue the position.

In almost all mortgage deeds there will be a clause making it clear that the proceeds of insurance are to be available to the mortgagee. In fact in standard bank mortgage forms there is a requirement that the money received shall be utilised towards making good the damage or towards the discharge of the mortgage debt. Generally this will be an option available to the bank.

Whilst dealing with the practical aspects, it is appropriate to mention that there is an arrangement between banks and members of the British Insurance Association by which insurance companies in the Group inform a bank if a policy, of which they have a notice of the bank's interest, is not renewed. The practice of most banks is to give notice of their interest in a fire policy. Some may occasionally insist upon it being in joint names of the mortgagor and mortgagee. Where there is a freeholder and leaseholder interested then the obligations of the lessee are dependent upon the terms of the lease, although normally it is possible for a banker mortgagee of leasehold interest to give notice effectively of his interest. In practice an insurance company will normally seek a discharge from all parties concerned and the actual utilisation of the money is a matter of negotiation.

The gist of the problem, however, is the rights in the circumstances of a bank against an insurance company. It is provided by the Law of Property Act, Section 108(3) as follows :

All money received on an insurance of mortgaged property against loss or damage by fire or otherwise effected under this Act, or any enactment replaced by this Act, or on an insurance for the maintenance of which the mortgagor is liable under the mortgage deed, shall, if the mortgagee so requires, be applied by the mortgagor in making good the loss or damage in respect of which the money is received.

As mentioned, such a clause appears in the standard form of bank mortgage. The rights of the mortgagee are further indicated by Sub-Section 4 of the Law of Property Act, as follows :

Without prejudice to any obligation to the contrary imposed by law, or by special contract, a mortgagee may require that all money received on an insurance of mortgaged property against loss or damage by fire or otherwise effected under this Act, or any enactment replaced by this Act, or on an insurance for the maintenance of which the mortgagor is liable under the mortgage deed, be applied in or towards the discharge of the mortgage money.

In the case of *Halifax Building Society* v. *Keighly* (1931) 2 K.B. 248 there was an insurance in joint names and also an insurance separately effected by the mortgagor. Accordingly the two insurance companies paid the parties proportionately and it was held that the society could not recover from the mortgagor the policy monies he had received separately.

In the normal course of events, however, notice given to and acknowledged by an insurance company will be sufficient. There has been no case argued before the courts in which a mortgagee failed to assert his rights to fire insurance monies where the fire insurance company had notice of the interest of the mortgagee. It is obviously, however, desirable to include the specific clause which is more or less standard in bank mortgage forms, to which reference has been made above.

It was held in *Sinnott* v. *Bowden* (1912) 2 Ch. 414 that a mortgagee could insist on rebuilding in such circumstances and, in addition, that a creditor of the mortgagor seeking to serve garnishee proceedings on the insurance company concerned could not obtain priority over the mortgagee. The difficulties arising where a number of parties have interest in the insurance claim can be seen from the *General Accident Fire & Life Assurance Corporation Ltd.* v. *Midland Bank Ltd.* (1942) 2 K.B. 388 where there were both buildings and plant that were the subject of a claim, there being a joint policy in the name of the bank and the freeholder and the lease-holder. In that case money was received in circumstances where the insurance company might not otherwise have been bound to pay because of the way in which the fire was started. It was a case in which the insurance company sought unsuccessfully to obtain repayment of money received by the bank and the freeholder. Nevertheless there were a number of comments in the judgment of the Master of the Rolls in which it was suggested that where two or three parties take out a joint policy there are really two or three *separate* contracts of insurance. This stems from the underlying basis that one does not insure a property against fire, but one insures a person's interest against his loss as a consequence of fire.

As to the specific question, it is indeed very difficult to see any grounds upon which the company could avoid paying twice if the monies have not been used to rebuild the house and it has not also become bank security. There are certain basic principles of equity to the effect that – even although there is only a contingent right to future monies – notice given by an equitable assignee cannot be ignored without risk of a second claim against a party paying away from a fund and ignoring the notice.

5 : A matured life policy

Mr X, a salaried Civil Servant, borrows £1,000 from his bank on loan account to buy a new car. Repayment is agreed at £25 monthly. As security, two policies on the life of Mr X are charged to the bank. The policies are £500 with profits maturing in 12 months and £250 with profits maturing in 7 years. The amounts inserted in the limitation clauses on the mortgages are £600 and £300 respectively.

Twelve months later the insurance company send to the bank a receipt form for the maturity monies which is completed and returned by the bank. Shortly afterwards a cheque for £700 is received. This is credited to the loan account which extinguishes the debt; and the loan account is closed. Mr X is then advised.

One week later a cheque for £700 is presented. As the balance of the current account is £25, an attempt is made to contact the customer. It is learned that he has been abroad for two weeks and cannot be reached. The cheque is returned marked 'Refer to Drawer'. One week later Mr X returns and, learning what has happened, sues the bank for wrongfully dishonouring his cheque. Discuss the bank's position.

The main point is that the policy *or its proceeds* was the bank's security. The giving of security, if required, is part of the loan contract between banker and customer and, as always, the retention of the security cannot be disputed by the customer without the repayment of the banker.

The other difficulties on the fringe of the problem are also of considerable interest : the possibility of making demand notwithstanding the references to repayment over a period; the right of set-off of surplus proceeds, if required, notwithstanding the limitation on the charge; and the right of appropriation of money received. The material point, however, was that the right to treat £600 of the £700 as security accrued to the bank because of the charge of the policy.

Although the situation in this problem – which, of course, should never have arisen in practice – admits of a reasonably straightforward solution, it has a number of interesting side issues.

Admittedly, it is difficult to understand why the *bankers* agreeing to the loan – which at £25 per month would take four years to repay

– and taking a security maturing in 1 year covering the major part of the borrowing, did not make specific arrangements to deal with the appropriation of the policy monies: as to by how much they were to reduce the loan. The bank would be bound by those arrangements; and the answer would turn on whether they had been properly observed, in that the terms of the mortgage may be deemed varied to this extent.

It must be assumed, however, that the bank made no such arrangements.

We can ask the following questions:

(*i*) Is the bank entitled to the policy monies?

(*ii*) Can the monies be applied to the loan account in this manner?

(*iii*) Is it necessary to make Mr X aware of the position?

(*i*) The bank is entitled to the policy monies; the policy has been properly assigned. The right to recover, however, is limited to £600 and it is sometimes considered that a banker's lien is barred to any remainder because of this specific provision. The mortgage may provide for certain additional expenses that may be recovered. The normal form allows for some items, *e.g.*, the cost of stamping, payment of premiums, to keep the security 'alive'. This situation illustrates, therefore, the importance of proper initial assessment to ensure the limitation is sufficient. The bank would appear to have exceeded its authority here by £100 and should account to Mr X accordingly.

(*ii*) The loan account is repayable on demand. Demand has not been made and there is no reason why it should have been, or will be, as the repayments are being regularly made. The policy monies cannot be applied to the loan account, but should now be the subject of discussion. In the meantime they should be held on a separate account as a security (as to £600 at any rate), because they now represent the policy; and the bank's right to them *as security* holds good. Once again the bank would seem to have acted incorrectly here.

(*iii*) Although notice to Mr X would be necessary for the reasons mentioned in (*ii*), it is not pertinent to the matter of the returned cheque; and it may indeed have been sufficient to write, as the bank did, to the customer's last known address.

The points have not been explored in any detail, because it is plain that without agreement by the bank only £100 at most will now be due to Mr X's current account; and this would have been insufficient to meet the cheque he has drawn. Although there is no doubt that he could not support an action based on these facts, he would have every right to be annoyed with a bank that has acted so clumsily throughout.

158

Part eight : Companies

The first thing to appreciate regarding a company is that it is a separate legal entity. Secondly, its powers and objects are limited by its Memorandum of Association. Its Articles of Association contain rules for its internal management, but so long as there is nothing apparent to the contrary a third party is entitled to presume that all that purports to have been done has been properly done. That is to say that resolutions have been passed where they are certified by the chairman as having been passed and that a document has been sealed in front of two witnesses where they have so indicated.

As to the specific questions :

Question 1
This question gave rise to a considerable amount of correspondence, but it is still thought that the answer is correct.

Question 2
The concept of a group banking account has much attraction to company accountants, but whilst there is no reason why it should not be operated very considerable care is needed in practice.

Question 3
Usually the mere intimation of the existence of a floating charge in favour of a mortgagee, especially in favour of a bank, has the practical effect of causing judgment creditors who were attempting to seize assets to give way.

Question 4
Solicitors' undertakings are one of the most useful mechanisms available to bankers and it has to be borne in mind that the Law Society has agreed specific forms with the Committee of London Clearing Bankers which should be used in all except the most unusual circumstances.

Question 5
This question has a very practical note of caution: if there is any doubt as to whether the company may have an interest, then not only

should the company be asked to give a charge on that interest, but registration should be effected if the item taken as security comes within the descriptions of Section 95 of the Companies Act 1948.

Question 6
This question reflects circumstances that recur far too often. As will be seen from the recent case quoted in the footnote of the answer, the courts often solve the problem rather on the lines of a partnership dispute.

Question 7
This answer is very much a warning, although legislation against tax avoidance by independent contractors providing labour has much reduced the popularity of the system.

1 : Fraud by a signatory on a company's account

The XYZ Co Ltd kept an account with the A branch of the Northtown Bank Ltd and arrangements were made for the company to draw wages at the B branch of the same bank to the extent of £750 in any one week, which the secretary later requested in writing be extended to £1,000. It transpired that the managing director had signed cheques in blank on the presumption of the continuance of the £750 limit; these the fraudulent secretary completed for £1,000 and pocketed the difference. Is the bank liable to the company?

Where the problem is difficult the best method of attempting a solution is to examine the various aspects and then endeavour to evaluate their respective merits with a view to seeking the solution that may be expected from a court hearing.

The first point for consideration is the mandate. When XYZ Co Ltd opened an account at the Northtown Bank there will have been a board resolution. At least the bank will receive a certificate that a resolution has been passed and, irrespective of whether or not such a meeting took place, is entitled to presume that it was properly done. This is so long as the mandate does not conflict with the terms of the Articles of Association. The mandate may refer only to the payment of cheques and bills; on the other hand it may relate specifically to other instructions given to the bank by the customer. If this or any other general wording is used there is a *prima facie* requirement that any instructions regarding the opening of a credit – whether it be a documentary credit or a clean drawing arrangement – should also be given in accordance with that mandate; that is to say that two signatories would be required to change any existing instructions; at first sight it would appear that the bank has acted without the necessary authority and is responsible for the consequences. Despite the other important factors discussed below this is probably the true answer. If the mandate makes no reference to the giving of instructions to the bank in relation to matters other than the drawing of the cheques, which is unlikely, there is probably some difference in that the function may be a

161

L

ministerial one normally falling within the authority of a secretary, unless there has been the contrary stipulation as there would be in most mandates.

There are however other aspects that may be argued strongly and perhaps even successfully on the part of the bank. First there is the principle of estoppel. That is that where one person represents to another that a certain state of affairs exists (although that is not the case) and another person acts upon such representation to his detriment, then the person who made the representation cannot come into court and rely upon the true state of affairs. To summarise the principle, it is the consequences of 'holding out'. Now when the bank has accepted an unauthorised instruction for the increased amount of the credit the problem is a little difficult, since the subsequent drawing by the company on a properly signed cheque is not the *original* cause of the company's loss. It is however a proximate cause. Furthermore the cheque is paid in accordance with the mandate. The material point is whether the bank can regard the subsequent event as preventing the company from denying that the secretary's instructions were good. An estoppel does not need to have been before the earlier event, as can be seen from the case of *Brown* v. *Westminster Bank* (THE BANKERS' MAGAZINE November and December, 1964) where the representatives of the customer prevented previous forgeries being set up. This then is a line of defence which would be adopted by any banker litigating the point.

Whether this possible contention could be maintained is very doubtful because there has to have been a representation from the company. It may have been different had the cheque been signed by the director after the amount had been inserted. Even then the position would perhaps not be entirely beyond dispute.

A further thought that occurs as to possible defence might be if there had been a course of business that was binding upon the company. It is true that there may have been a number of occasions upon which these cheques for £750 had been encashed; but, unless the correspondence on the files of the bank shows that the arrangement had become known to the board or at least to the director who signed the cheques under the misapprehension, there is little prospect of success for the bank if it adopts this particular line of defence.

Yet a further possible contention might be on the grounds of contributory negligence. Contributory negligence is normally, however, relevant only where an action is being brought, in tort, that is to say, is

162

where someone has a right arising irrespective of a contract. A common example is where someone is knocked down by a car and both parties are in some measure negligent, in which event the responsibility is divided. In the present instance there is no doubt that the relationship between the bank and its customer is contractual; thus although the customer has in some measure been negligent it is doubtful whether any part of the responsibility of the bank can thereby be avoided. It is true that where a cheque is drawn in such a way as to permit an amount to be altered and the form of the drawing has been careless to such an extent as to facilitate such alteration the paying banker has no responsibility. This is different from the position where there is negligence relating to the forgery of a cheque, as is known only too well. Where a signature on a cheque has been forged as a consequence of negligence of the customer, the negligence is not associated with the actual drawing of the cheque and is, therefore, regarded as too remote.

The better view, therefore, of this difficult question, is that, in the absence of special circumstances which to put them at their highest is that the board was aware of the change in amount of the credit facility or to put them at their lowest is that the director who signed the cheques was aware of such change, there is no defence for the bank*.

* The above answer produced considerable correspondence but is thought to be the better view.

2 : One banking account for a group of companies

*Mr X, who is the chairman of the principal company in a group
forming an excellent connection of the local branch of Brown's Bank,
wishes to have only one banking account for the whole of the group,
which sometimes borrows money. What answer should be given?*

The evident complication involved in the administration of such accounts is likely to make most bankers very hesitant before they become
involved. The general utilisation of such a method of conducting banking accounts might well be opposed by the banks as a whole because of
administrative difficulties. There is no law requiring a company to
keep a bank account although it must of course keep accounts and
produce profit and loss accounts and balance sheets. Only in a group
really well organised from an accounting standpoint would customers
find that the burden of the proposal was not overwhelming.
The short answer is that Brown's Bank can assist Mr X in his request
to have only one banking account for the group of companies by opening a joint account in the name of all of them. This is, however, subject to the undermentioned points being in order :

(*a*) The Memoranda and Articles of Association of all the companies
in the group should be examined and the following ascertained :

(*i*) In each case are both the directors' and companies' borrowing
powers sufficient to cover the maximum borrowing likely to be
seen on the joint account plus any other money the company
in question may have borrowed from any other source? If any
of the companies have inadequate borrowing powers, the Memorandum of Association may be altered by special resolution unless such
alteration is prohibited by the memorandum itself (Companies Act 1948,
Sections 5 & 23). If the directors' powers are inadequate the safest
thing would be to get the Articles of Association altered, again by
special resolution. Alternatively, if a regulation similar to Table A
Article 79 of the Companies Act 1948 is included an ordinary resolution in general meeting will be sufficient. In connection with
this point, Brown's Bank should obtain certified copies of the appropriate resolutions in any case where it is necessary for them to be passed.

164

(*ii*) Is there anything contained therein which might preclude the company from being a party to a joint account with joint and several liability? Brown's Bank must obviously satisfy itself on this point as, if the answer was 'Yes' in the case of any of the companies, in the event of the winding-up of those companies any debit balance would be irrecoverable from their liquidators.

(*iii*) Are all the companies empowered to give guarantees? This point is raised as it may well be argued in any liquidation that being party to a joint account with joint and several liability is tantamount to giving a guarantee, especially when one considers (as will be explained below) any debit balance on the account may have been created by the other companies in the group, *i.e.*, a company may be a party to the account without actually drawing any cheques or paying in credits.

(*b*) Provided the points under (*a*) are satisfactory, Brown's Bank may proceed further and request that each of the companies in the group pass resolutions which, in addition to setting the usual arrangements as to who may sign/endorse cheques, bills, etc., on behalf of the company, should embody the following points:

(*i*) That Brown's Bank be authorised to open a joint account in the names of the companies in the group and that one of the companies in the group (usually the parent) be authorised to confirm additions and deletions from the joint account. This enables a new company to come into the joint account or for one to leave without the necessity of all the companies in the group passing resolutions.

(*ii*) That such additions or deletions be made without the necessity of opening a fresh account. If this clause was not included when a company, say, left the joint account it would have to be broken, if in debit, to preserve the bank's right against the other companies, *i.e.*, Clayton's Case could operate against the bank and the bank's right against a particular company be extinguished, though they would be liable for any debt they created after the relevant date.

(*iii*) That each company be authorised to draw cheques, bills, etc., on the joint account. This enables any one company to draw on the account.

(*iv*) That Brown's Bank is authorised to collect cheques, bills, etc., drawn in favour of any one of the companies for the credit of the joint account. This is self-explanatory but it ensures the bank will receive the benefit of statutory protection contained in Sections 3 & 4 of the Cheques Act 1957 without the necessity of obtaining endorsements.

(v) That Mr X (or some other official of the company in question) be authorised to sign an agreement in the form produced to the meeting which, for identification purposes, is signed in the margin by the chairman of the meeting. The agreement makes the company jointly and severally liable for any debt on the joint account and contains a provision for the companies to give notice of determination which, in the event, would, of course, mean breaking the account to preserve the liability. As it is under hand, the agreement is signed over a 6d stamp.

We are not told whether the group consists of a parent company and its wholly-owned subsidiaries but, if it does, it will almost certainly be in order for each of the companies to pass the resolution at a Directors' meeting as they are unlikely to have any personal interest. If the formation of the group is anything less than this, then the possibility of the personal interest of a Director becomes quite strong. To take a simple example, Mr X himself may well be a shareholder in two of the companies in the group, say XY Ltd and XZ Ltd. As stated above, a company joining the account is to all intents and purposes guaranteeing debts which may be created by another party. Mr X would, therefore, have an interest at both the board meetings of XY Ltd, and XZ Ltd for it is a widely accepted point that, when it is proposed that one company gives a guarantee for the liabilities of another and a director of the first is also a shareholder of the second, there is a conflict of interests.

If circumstances such as these do prevail with any of the companies, it will be necessary in those cases for the resolution to be passed either by an independent quorum or at a general meeting of shareholders, unless the Articles of Association provide interested directors may vote on matters of this nature.

If all the above may be and is carried out, Mr X will have just one bank account for his group of companies on which any one of them may draw. It should, however, be made clear to him that each of the companies is liable for the whole of any debit balance which may appear.

3 : Bank holding floating charge ousting judgment creditor

X Limited has given the R Bank a floating charge for all liabilities of the company to the bank. The bank learns that the company has had a judgment given against it and that the bailiffs have arrived at the company's premises. What should the bank do?

It is necessary to appreciate two important facets of this problem before examining the steps to be taken by the bank: first, the nature of a floating charge and, secondly, how bailiffs come to be in possession.

A floating charge is a mortgage given by a limited company of the whole of its assets; for obvious reasons it does not mean that the chargee (or mortgagee) – that is to say the bank – is in possession of the property, any more than would be the case if a fixed (or ordinary) mortgage of a house is taken. Although the floating charge covers the book debts, stock in trade, plant and machinery as well as all the real and leasehold property, the company continues to trade normally and has control over all its assets. This may and often does continue for many years until the bank is repaid. Occasionally, however, the bank may be dissatisfied as to the conduct of the account or of the company's business. The remedy is then open to the bank to take control. As with any other security a necessary preliminary is to make demand for repayment, for that the customer will repay on demand is the condition of all bank borrowing and security. Once demand is made the next day (or perhaps later the same day) the bank may appoint a receiver. In practice this is usually a chartered accountant, with some knowledge of the trade in which the company is engaged. The appointment may be made under hand and merely says – almost in so many words – that the money secured by the charge has become due and that Mr X has been appointed receiver. With such document the receiver may take over and run or sell the business to the best advantage of the bank.

Most readers will have been aware of much of the foregoing but the history of events leading up to the entry of the bailiffs will be a different matter.

The next aspect to consider is the possession by the bailiffs. When

167

there is a legal action and the result is that the defendant is directed to pay money to the plaintiff this often is only the beginning of the plaintiff's difficulties. Sometimes the defendant may pay the plaintiff and satisfy the judgment but in other instances, either because he has not the available cash or because he has not even the assets to produce sufficient cash, the defendant does nothing. If he intends to appeal against the judgment he will often succeed in getting a 'stay of execution' so that it cannot be enforced, but otherwise it is obvious that the law has to provide remedies to enable the plaintiff to obtain satisfaction if the defendant is contumacious or slow to take the steps to realise sufficient assets to make the payment. It is true that the plaintiff can issue a bankruptcy notice by which there is an 'available act of bankruptcy' if the defendant does not pay the amount of the judgment within eight days. This however involves formalities of presenting a petition and moreover means the equal distribution of the debtor's property among all creditors. Thus if the plaintiff knows of assets and is not confident that the debtor can pay 20s. in the £1 in the forced sale circumstances of bankruptcy he will seek to satisfy his judgment from known assets. The method with which bankers are most closely acquainted is that of garnishee proceedings, by which where a debt is owing to the defendant the judgment creditor may obtain satisfaction by the service of a garnishee order *nisi* which, subject to examination by the court, if any of the parties so wishes, is made absolute and sufficient money paid by the bank from the credit balance to satisfy the judgment. The court, incidentally, will not re-open the case but merely satisfy itself as to whether cash is due to the debtor and a valid judgment in existence. Similarly if the debtor has land or shares the court will make a charging order. Where the judgment creditor knows of chattels in existence then a writ of *fieri facias* (commonly known as *fi. fa.*) is obtained. This enables the sheriff's officers to put their representatives in possession and after eight days remove, advertise and sell the goods seized for the benefit of the judgment creditor. The foregoing principles apply whether the judgment debtor is an individual or a company, but the details and application of the principles are different because an individual is made bankrupt and a company is wound up.

Turning to the question whether the bank is mortgagee under a floating charge it is necessary to appoint a receiver before the sheriff's officer has sold (or at all events before he has parted with the proceeds of sale). The position is covered by sections 325 and 326 of the Com-

168

panies Act, 1948, which refer to the 'completion of execution' by the sheriff. This is the stage by which a holder of a floating charge must appoint a receiver. Obviously the quicker the better. Usually but not always the bank will learn that the bailiffs have taken possession of stock, machinery or other chattels belonging to the company, but sometimes this is not so. Of course, machinery frequently belongs to hire purchase companies and is not available to the judgment creditor (as with a private individual, furniture if not belonging to such a company is claimed as the property of the debtor's wife). So far as the bank is concerned all that has to be done is the making of demand and the appointment of a receiver. In dire urgency even the manager if able to bind the bank for that purpose could appoint the receiver by writing out the appointment. It is given to the chartered accountant or other person appointed who goes to the premises and directs the bailiffs to leave because it is the bank's property. Frequently the mere knowledge of the existence of a bank floating charge will cause the sheriff's officers to give up possession.

M

4 : Solicitors' undertaking on behalf of a company

A bank agrees to lend money to company X for the acquisition of property A against an undertaking by solicitors to hold the deeds on behalf of the bank pending the completion of a formal mortgage. What risks are involved for the bank? In particular, what is the position of the bank if a petition for the liquidation of the company is presented before the formal mortgage is completed?

At the outset it is to be emphasised that this question has no reference to the honesty and integrity of solicitors, which can be taken for granted almost invariably. In the very rare and exceptional instance of a banker suffering through a solicitor failing through inadvertence or for any other reason to fulfil an undertaking, resort may be had to the fund established by the Law Society for such contingencies.

One risk where a company is concerned is a risk that arises when any other form of fixed mortgage is taken in respect of a company's property. If there are floating charges (or debentures) outstanding, this may prevent the company from giving a fixed mortgage. Notice of the charge, which will be registered in the Companies Registry, has been held not to be notice of a restriction it contained. This was the decision in two cases half a century or more ago (*English & Scottish Mercantile Investment Co. v. Brunton* (1892 29B. 700) and *Re Valletort Sanitary Steam Laundry Co.* (1903 2 Ch. 654). It is, however, the practice of some holders of floating charges to have recorded on Form 47 or Form 47A – on which the registration is recorded – a note of the restriction against the company creating fixed charges. Where there has been a search it will be difficult for the party searching to allege that he has no notice, although there is no decision directly on the point. The case of *Re Mechanisation (Eaglescliffe) Ltd.* (1964 3 A.E.R. 840) is a reminder that a searcher *cannot* rely upon details as to the maximum amount of such debentures. Thus although the risk of a restriction preventing a charge being created by the solicitors' undertaking is perhaps small, it is one that a banker cannot ignore. If the circumstances indicate that the company is pressed it will be desirable for the aspect to be pursued to avoid possible controversy, if for no more serious reason.

The more serious risk, however, is that indicated by the question itself which alludes to the contingency of liquidation. The undertaking by solicitors to hold deeds is the equivalent of the deeds being held by the bank and is thus a mortgage without written charge. As such, involving an interest in land, the charge created by the deposit of deeds (of which the solicitors have constructive possession on behalf of the bank) requires registration if it is to be good against a liquidator or a competing mortgagee. It does not mean that the company itself is not bound by the charge. However, if the liquidation has supervened then, although the solicitor implements his undertaking and sends the deeds to the bank, they may be claimed by the liquidator just the same as if they had been deposited with the bank and it had omitted to register. From a practical standpoint, therefore, a banker can rely upon such a position when he is satisfied that the company is financially strong and that liquidation in the near future can be entirely disregarded, but otherwise he should consider the merits of registration in the light of the circumstances generally – his other security, his measure of dependence upon the mortgage of the deeds, the time likely to elapse before there will be a formal charge or bridgeover-finance will be repaid. A solicitor himself would not normally object but where there is *not* intended to be a permanent charge but there is merely a bridgeover, a company having no outstanding charges on its register may be very concerned as to its credit generally. Sometimes there is a solution in that the whole transaction is completed within twenty-one days, which, of course, is the time during which a holder may register his charge. The question is a matter for the banker's discretion but involving a contingency of which he should be aware. It is of course desirable to explain one's intention to the solicitor before effecting registration, which is done rarely in practice—usually only if the mortgagor's credit is fragile or very large amounts are involved.

5 : Rival claims of a company and its director to mortgaged property

Grocers Limited, which has three directors, has an overdrawn account with you, and you are pressing for a reduction or a security. Smith, a director, deposits the lease of a shop occupied by the company, which is in his name. You think that he may hold this lease as trustee for the company, but he insists that it is his property. He declines to sign a memorandum or deposit, saying that the deposit of the lease with the bank is sufficient.

A week later you receive a letter from the Downtown Bank asking for the lease to be sent to them, enclosing an authority signed by the other two directors. Your mandate is for any one director to sign cheques and withdraw securities. You discover that the Downtown Bank also has an overdrawn account in the name of Grocers Limited, and they too are pressing for repayment. What action should you take, and what could you do to strengthen your position?

Where there is a complex question it may often simplify the approach if it is taken piecemeal. On this basis the first thought is that although the lease is said to belong to the company by the other two directors they may not be correct in their contention. The history of the matter will show how the lease came in the first place to have been in the name of Smith. There must have been a reason. Either he may have been the original owner and have sold it to the company, alternatively the lessors may have demanded a personal lessee, although the latter problem is normally overcome by a director or some other individual becoming surety. Again, there may be a suggestion – possibly supported by correspondence or similar evidence – that Smith borrowed money from the company to buy the lease.

Thus the first question to be answered is as to the position of the bank should it eventuate to be the property of Smith – admittedly unlikely but not excluded by the terms of the question. The bank has no evidence of the purpose of the deposit and the borrowing is in the name of Grocers Limited not Smith – so the equitable mortgage is not implied by the mere possession, as is the case where the borrowing is in the name of the owner. On the other hand, if a deposit of deeds cannot be explained away by any other reason, then it is just possible for the bank to set itself up as equitable mortgagee even for a third party liability. It is difficult in practice but the possibility can be supported by the decision of *Bozon* v. *Williams* (1829 3 Y. and J. 150).

All the foregoing comments relate to the contingency of the lease belonging to Smith. It may be, however, that it can be proved that Smith held the lease on behalf of the company. The question of registration against the company is not relevant except where the company is known to be or thought possibly to be the beneficial owner of the property. This was obviously not the case, although in practice it is prudent to effect registration if there appears to be doubt.

The gist of the matter is whether the bank had notice of the interest of the company. The occupation of the property by the company may be suggested as notice that Smith was a nominee, but this is by no means conclusive. Often a company will take a short tenancy of a property from a director and in the absence of other relevant evidence this would not adversely affect the position of the bank as mortgagee. Where a person purchases a property and leaves the title in the name of someone else he runs the risk of being regarded as negligent and unable to refute the contentions of a third party who relies upon title deeds in the name of someone other than the owner. This is not quite the same but the principle of negligence and the responsibility of having clothed that person with 'indicia' of title is pertinent.

There is yet a further possible answer available in the authority – if not inconsistent with the Articles of Association – given to Smith to withdraw securities. It may be that this could imply their deposit, although this aspect depends on the precise wording of the mandate. Thus it can be claimed, even if the company could establish that the bank had notice of trust, the deeds were left with the bank with the company's authority. At all events the physical deposit cannot be effected by the company other than through a director or an employee. To strengthen its position the bank should inform the company that demand will be made for repayment if the deposit is not confirmed. It would be well to take a formal legal mortgage and register this at the Companies Registry. If the other directors are not agreeable then after demand the account should be stopped, subject to provision for outstanding cheques and commitments. It is perhaps open to doubt whether this last-mentioned proviso is necessary because the security tendered originally for the company's account – on which basis the facility was provided – is later found *not* to be valid.

173

6 : A petition because of directors' quarrels

X Ltd has a credit account with Town Bank Ltd. Its two directors,
A and B, each of whom own fifty shares, are men of considerable
substance and reputation in the town. A dispute arises between them
and A presents a petition for the liquidation of the company. What
should the bank do with regard to the necessity for the company to
continue banking business, bearing in mind that it is thought that the
hearing of the petition will be adjourned for three or four weeks because,
although the petition has been presented by A as a creditor, the court
will recognise that basically there is a quarrel.

The first thing to appreciate is that we are concerned with a compulsory winding-up. This follows from the fact that there is a petition
presented. There are two other kinds of winding-up : a members' voluntary winding-up and a creditors' winding-up. A members' winding-
up is where there has been a declaration of solvency and
for practical purposes the control is in the hands of the shareholders
and directors of the old company. The second kind is where the company is insolvent but the creditors are willing that a liquidator shall
be appointed to act and control the position with the help of the Committee of Inspection, he being subject to the decisions of the creditors
generally.

A banker's concern with the presentation of the petition is the conduct of the account pending the making of an order for the winding-up.
By section 229 (2) of the 1948 Act 'the winding up of a company
by the court shall be deemed to commence at the time of the presenta-
of the petition for the winding-up'. So that from the time of the
presentation of a winding-up petition and before a winding-up
order is made, the company is still in existence and can
carry on business; but as the winding-up order dates back to the
presentation of the petition one must consider Section 227 that 'any
disposition of the property . . . after the commencement of the winding-
up is void, unless the court otherwise orders'. The object of this provision is to prevent, during the period which must elapse before a
petition can be heard, the improper alienation and dissipation of the

174

property of a company about to fold up. The court can, however, sanction transactions in the ordinary course of business – otherwise the presentation of the petition, whether well or ill-founded, would paralyse X, Ltd's trade (*Re Steane's (Bournemouth) Ltd.* 1950). The legal cases tend to be in favour of the parties who act in good faith and with the honest intention of benefiting the company. This is of little help to the banker who may be faced with cheques drawn on the company's account, for he is not to know if they are genuine transactions or dissipation of the company's property, nor is it his duty to inquire. Any transaction which would be void in bankruptcy as a fraudulent preference is also void in a winding-up if made within six months of the commencement of the winding-up.

Whilst the problem is difficult for a banker when the petition is presented, because of the inability of the company to pay its debts, the situation is even more embarrassing where a petition has been presented by a shareholder on the basis that for some other reason – such as the company being conducted to the detriment of a minority – it is claimed that it should be put into liquidation. In the first instance the banker will normally pay cash to the company, but not pay third party cheques. This position is understood commercially. On the other hand in the second instance the petition may basically have stemmed from a dispute between directors relating to the affairs of the company or even a quarrel outside the affairs of the company of a more personal nature; it is this kind of petition that is likely to be adjourned. During this interim period the banker, who may be affording finance to the company, is embarrassed because there may be an impasse bringing the affairs of the company to a standstill. In such circumstances the first course, practically speaking, is to try to bring the parties together with a view to *modus vivendi* being established so that the business does not go to rack and ruin. Generally it will be accepted by the solicitors, if not by their clients, that such a step cannot but be of advantage to both. On the other hand a personal feud may cause a client to refuse to follow the suggestions made by his solicitors. In such event if one of the directors is a man of considerable substance the banker may find some help, if not a complete solution, in taking a personal indemnity from the director in question and paying cheques with such protection.

The leading case relating to the payment of cheques during this interim period is that of *D. B. Evans (Bilston), Ltd.* v. *Barclays Bank Ltd.* (*The Times*, 17 February, 1961).

In *D.B. Evans (Bilston) Ltd.* v. *Barclays Bank* (*The Times*, 17 Feb. 1961), however, the bank refused to pay out after the filing of a winding-up petition which was presented against the plaintiffs, their customers, on 16 January, 1961. On the same day an appliction was made to the Court under Section 206 of the Companies Act, 1948, for a scheme of arrangement to be prepared. The company were public works contractors employing 600 workmen with a weekly wage bill of £8,000. The Court adjourned the winding-up proceedings pending the sanctioning of the scheme. The bank allowed the plaintiffs to withdraw credit balances which were in existence prior to the filing of the winding-up petition (subject to the retention of a sum which had been garnisheed) but informed them that the credit balance of a newly opened No. 4 account (instituted shortly after the filing of the winding-up petition) and the proceeds of any further cheques which might be paid in for the credit of this account would be frozen pending the outcome of the winding-up petition.

In saying this the bank had in contemplation the terms of Section 227 of the Companies Act, 1948.

The bank feared that if they paid out money to their company customer in these circumstances they might be called upon again at a later date to pay an equivalent amount to the liquidator.

The company in the next few weeks received cheques payable to themselves but could not turn them into cash, knowing that if they paid them into their bank for collection, the proceeds would be frozen. They had no other cash resources and were, therefore, faced with the prospect of having to discharge their employees and cease work. They therefore brought an action against the bank claiming damages for breach of contract and asking for an injunction to restrain the defendant bank from refusing to honour the company's cheques to the extent that the company's banking account was in credit. In the Court of Appeal it was said for the company that a banker, unless he had a special term in his contract, was bound to pay his customer's cheques to the limit of the amount in credit, unless there was some legal bar. It was submitted that there was no legal bar in the present case.

The defendant bank relied on Section 227. After hearing legal argument the Court adjourned to allow the parties to confer. Before adjourning, Sellers, L.J., asked whether some limited arrangement might not be made, not absolutely restricted to wages, but on as stringent terms as the bank desired. His Lordship could not see that the bank would be running any risk.

176

A scheme was then agreed between the parties to the effect that the company should pay in to the credit of their account such cheques, payable to them, as they wished, and the bank would honour cheques to the extent of the credit balance from time to time, provided that such cheques were drawn to cash or to the company's order and were properly certified by a director of the company and a solicitor or a chartered accountant as necessary to be disbursed for the purpose of carrying on its business. If within the following three weeks the scheme under Section 206 of the Companies Act, 1948, was approved by the creditors, the above order would continue until the adjourned hearing of the winding-up petition.

The Court duly gave its sanction to this arrangement and accordingly was not required to resolve the question of law arising. The case, however, instanced the difficulties in which both banker and customer are placed in the interim period between the presentation of a petition and the possible making of a winding-up order.

Thus, turning again to the specific question, the bank is under no obligation to continue the banking business other than by way of payment of cash to the company. It is, of course, assumed that the quarrel has not caused the company to be unable to draw cheques owing to the absence of a director's signature. One director may be able to stop cheques on which his signature appears, but normally he will not be able to alter the mandate which has come from the Board. Although each case depends on its merits, the principles are outlined above.*

* The point again came before the courts when it will be seen appreciably the need for intervention where there is an impasse (See *Legal Decisions* The Bankers' Magazine, July 1969, p. 27.) Also, in the case of *Grays Inn Construction Co Ltd* (1980) 1. A.E.R 814, the need for caution by a banker is further evidenced.

7 : A wages preferential claim

On 1 June a petition is presented to the Court for the compulsory winding-up of a company. The company has an overdraft and the borrowing (on that date), including interest, amounts to £10,000. No security is held other than the balance of account guarantee of the directors.

The company is engaged in the construction of houses. Although no separate wages account is operated, cheques have been presented payable to wages. On inquiry it is ascertained that of three wages cheques, for £2,000 each, debited to the account on 7, 14 and 21 May, respectively, only £1,500 was paid to employees of the company; the remained was paid to a gang leader who then paid the men under his jurisdiction.

The bank decides to submit a preferential claim to the liquidator. The statement of the account for the last month is as follows:

XYZ Company Ltd. (£):

May 2		1,000	2,500 Cr.
5	12,000		9,500 Dr.
7 (Wages)	2,000		11,500 Dr.
10	3,500		15,000 Dr.
12		2,500	12,500 Dr.
14 (Wages)	2,000		14,500 Dr.
17		3,000	11,500 Dr.
19	1,000		12,500 Dr.
20		5,000	7,500 Dr.
21 (Wages)	2,000		9,500 Dr.
June 1	500		10,000 Dr.

Because of the operation of the Rule in Clayton's Case only the last five debits plus £1,000 from the wages cheque debited to the account on 7 May can constitute the balance of the account on 1 June, the commencement of winding up of the company.

For how much can the bank prove as a preferential creditor?

178

The first point of very practical interest is that despite there being no wages account a banker may claim as preferential creditor to the extent to which the advances made were made for the purpose of the payment of wages and have been used as such. For the sake of clarity and for the sake of ensuring the maximum amount of such claim it is desirable and customary for a separate wages account to be opened. Then the amount advanced is not repaid by credits into the account. A maximum of sixteen weeks' wages advances is kept upon the separate wages account. Frequently the extent of the bank's preferential claim will be less than the aggregate of the account. There are a number of reasons that can cause the acceptable amount of the claim to be less than the balance of the account. On the other hand – as distinct from instances given in the question – the balance of a separate wages account will not be reduced by credits into the account in accordance with the normal application of the rule in Clayton's case. This has clearly happened in the instance indicated above. But for the credits received it is apparent that the wages claim would have been greater. That is to say, if a wages account had been opened it would have been advantageous to the bank. Sometimes this precaution is omitted. On other occasions, however, the seriousness of the company's financial position is not recognised.

The second aspect concerns the instances in which reductions may be effected. A number of these should never arise. Cheques are drawn ostensibly for the purpose of wages and used to pay directors' fees, petty cash and various other payments not coming within the category. A further example is illustrated by the question and is supported by a reported decision of re C. W. & A. L. Hughes, Ltd. (1966 2 All ER 702). In that case a preferential claim was put forward but in fact the company had engaged a ganger, or, more elegantly, an independent contractor, to provide the labour. The company paid the money to the ganger who provided the men. It was he who paid them and they were in fact his servants. For this reason such payments have to be excluded since they were not in payment of wages due to a servant of the company. Incidentally, there is a maximum of £200 for each sixteen weeks which of itself will exclude in part wages of a number of employees. Again if an individual is a director, as distinct perhaps from managing director, he is not an employee and the money advanced to pay his fees has to be excluded.

The fundamental question is the extent to which a bank can prove as a preferential creditor. Clearly the wages payments of the 14 and 21

179

May each of £2,000 justifies a preferential claim on the basis that they were advances for the payment of wages to the extent that it was so used. The figure, we are told, was £1,500 in each case. This then leaves the cheque of the 7 May which, to the extent of £1,000 has been repaid by receipt of credits in. This point we are given in the question. We are told that £1,500 only of the £2,000 was used for wages. The answer required is a matter of some difficulty in that one has to determine whether a direct pro rata apportionment will be taken and £750 be recognised as a preferential, or whether the whole of the £1,000 will be recognised as preferential despite the fact that £500 of the total £2,000 used went to pay not wages but the independent director.

It has been decided in *re William Hall (Contractor), Ltd.* (1967 2 All ER, 1150), (*see* THE BANKERS' MAGAZINE, vol. CCV, Feb. 1968, p. 91, vol. CCIV, July 1967, p. 26–7) that a bank may use the proceeds of its security to repay first a non-preferential debt. It is true that a cheque received in reduction of an account is temporarily a bank security because a bank has a lien over the security. Nevertheless it is not thought that this is a complete answer. Otherwise there would be no doubt that the bank could appropriate the repayment, effected by the cheque paid in, to the non-preferential debt. This may in fact be the answer. However, there is another principle which is more likely to be held by a court to determine the question. That is that when someone pays money into a banking account he has a right to appropriate that money whether it be cash or proceeds of a cheque. Sometimes it is appropriated to the payment of another cheque. Where there is more than one account it may be appropriated, explicitly or implicitly, to the credit of the particular account. Where there is no express appropriation it is open to the bank to appropriate the money. The question then arises as to whether the bank has irrevocably appropriated the money received 'penny for penny' in reduction of the cheque upon the current account, or whether there is any residuary right of appropriation. There is no decided case on this particular issue, but it seems probable that the bank would be entitled to utilise the money as it wishes which, of course, would be in reduction of the non-preferential debt. Taken in conjunction with the principle enunciated in the case mentioned above is thought that this would be the probable result. In practice a banker usually manages to substantiate a claim on such a basis.

Part nine : Miscellaneous problems

The topics coming under this category reflect either the very unusual or modern development, such as credit transfers.

As to the specific questions:

Question 1

It has to be borne in mind that as yet the credit transfer has not come before the court. One hopes that it never may, but to ignore its legal implications would be extremely unwise.

Question 2

This is a reminder that all banks are not of the same financial integrity. Since presumably bankers payments will be confined to recognised banks within the meaning of the Banking Act 1979 and since they (as well as licensed deposit takers) are under the control of the Bank of England, it is now less likely that these circumstances will obtain—although insolvency of a foreign bank involving its London Branch is still a possibility that may stem from unwise transactions abroad.

Question 3

This is a more sophisticated question on credit transfers.

Question 4

This stems from the thought that inevitably credit transfers in practice will be issued on the strength of cheques drawn by the transferor and/ or third parties, despite inhibitions to the contrary. It is like paying against uncleared effects – officially discountenanced or discouraged, but a feature of daily life.

Question 5

This deals with an unusual situation, but the problem called for tact and legal knowledge.

Question 6

This is the one instance where the question is undoubtedly a figment of the imagination or at least coloured. Nevertheless the points of principle are very real and would be applicable in practice to perhaps the same events in less trite circumstances.

1 : Credit transfer and a dishonoured cheque

Bank A receives across the counter four credit transfers for onward transmission, one for rates, one for gas account, one for electricity account and one in payment of a hire purchase debt. All are for different banks and a cheque for the total, drawn on bank B, is given in payment, the person paying in stating that he cannot get to his own bank.

Three days later the cheque is received unpaid with the answer 'Refer to Drawer'. What action can bank A take to reimburse itself and what does it do with the cheque?

There is, of course, an official instruction that payments to provide the wherewithal for credit transfers should be in cash. As was also mentioned, no banker is going to be so pedantic as to decline to accept a cheque from a customer of his own branch because that is the same as cash or immediately can be ascertained as being so by reference to the ledger sheet. The next point, practically, is the good cheque tendered with the credit transfer drawn not on your own branch but on another and perhaps local branch of your bank, the customer being of impeccable repute. Here again few bankers would risk provoking such a drawer (and possibly also their fellow managers) by declining to regard his cheque as cash. In fact one might say that in some measure this stage of the problem can be equated to that of whether a cheque would be cashed for a particular drawer. All the precautions (and some of the risks) associated with the encashment of third party cheques are involved. At one extreme, a stranger with a cheque on another bank would be refused, as he would at the inn over the road. The circumstances and the amount determine the decision, but in the case of the cheque tendered for the credit transfer the minimisation of the risk is not so difficult and from the legal standpoint, the possibility of reimbursement is not so remote. Implicit in the working of the credit transfer system is the co-operation between bankers, as a number of correspondents emphasised, with the result that technicality is quite irrelevant. It is true that the legal position – as with all practical commercial problems – forms the basis upon which any compromise or settlement will be often achieved. This is nonetheless possible by reason of the basic legal position being difficult or in doubt, as is the case with some aspects of credit transfer. Perhaps deliberately, it seems that the system is to be permitted to develop, as has the banker-customer relationship generally, without at the outset there being any rigorously defined legal basis. As we shall see, it is left in some degree at least to the customers to establish their own legal position in relation with their debtors whom they are willing shall pay them through the system. In fact to a considerable extent it is open to them to create the precise basis of their legal relationship, not only with their own bankers, but also with those through whom the payment is to be made.

Reverting to the specific problem, a cheque drawn by a third party has been received so that four credit transfers shall be effected. That cheque, one is entitled to presume, will be payable either to the receiving banker or to the bearer, or perhaps to cash. Although in theory a cheque payable to a third party could be received, it is very unlikely that this would be the case, and in any event only if the payee was known, was undoubted, and had endorsed it. The cheque having been dishonoured, there is, of course, no doubt that the banker receiving it could sue the drawer if he made the payments requested *and* it was impossible for him to insist upon, or in some other way, achieve their recall. He is either the holder of a cheque payable to himself or payable to bearer. Even if it is payable to cash – and therefore not strictly a cheque – the only possible difference would be that the onus of proof that there was a good consideration would be on the banker, rather than the customer being faced with the burden of proving that there was none. The aspect is insignificant because proof would be easy and the receiving banker could demand payment, at least as an equitable assignee.

The more important and more difficult facet is whether the banker can in fact in the four cases recover the payments and whether he has a legal right to do so. Many answers indicated that in practice there would normally be time to recall the credits and/or that the other bankers would assist in this being done, without adverting to the legal position, which in any event they would often find perplexing. This does not however enable the answer to the problem to be given similarly without enquiry into 'the legal basis'.

The nub of the question is whether the receiving banker is the agent of the payer or of the ultimate recipient. The local Council, Gas Board, Electricity Company or hire purchase company may establish that relationship by the wording of the form they use. It may for example state that the money is to be paid to a bank 'as agent' for the local Council. The better view is that once this has been done the item received is handled by the bankers as agents for the ultimate recipient. As a consequence, the payer may not then say to the bankers that they are his agents and if he requests *must stop* a payment if they can. By way of corollary, if as in this instance the cheque is dishonoured, Bank A, the receiving banker, is able to say that he received the item as agent for the banker of the local Council (or other recipent) and that he is entitled to reimbursement in the ordinary way, just as if a credit had been paid for a customer's account, or for the customer of another branch or banker and had been dishonoured. There is the implied indemnity of principal to agent. The other possibility is that the receiving banker is agent for the person making the payment. In so far as the literature published by the Banks may amount to an open offer, that is, to anyone to accept, then the receiving banker is agent of the payer who can recall monies if they are in the hands or under direct or indirect control of the receiving banker. Similarly Bank A having made payment cannot as of right claim reimbursement should the money have reached the recipient.

The conclusion is subject to two other comments. First, if Bank A suffered a loss it is entitled to stand in the shoes of the person benefiting from its mistake. With the local Council, unless the ratepayer has quitted, recovery is probable by levying distress. With the Gas or Electricity Board payment might well be engendered by cutting off supply. Perhaps less hopefully, with the hire purchase company the item hired may be seized, sold and a surplus produced. These rights are theoretical, depending on the practical circumstances. Secondly, even although the receiving banker is not agent of the ultimate recipient, recovery on the general legal principle of money paid under mistake of fact should be examined. The law surrounding this subject is complicated but when a payment has been made and both the recipient and the payer have been under the same mistaken apprehension recovery is possible. There are however two important exceptions: where the recipient has altered his position in consequence, at all events if he has received as agent, and where payment has been made by a negotiable instrument that has actually been negotiated. These circumstances may not often apply, and if the facts are not clear the added legal complication would discourage litigation for recovery by Bank A unless it could establish that it was agent of the recipient as in the manner indicated in this answer.

184

2 : Dishonour of a banker's payment

XYZ Ltd, Anytown Branch, discount a bill drawn by its customer, Anyone Ltd, accepted by Brown Ltd, payable three months after sight at the London office of Merchant Bank ABC Ltd.

At maturity, the bill is presented for payment and a banker's payment is received in settlement from the Merchant bank drawn on their account with clearing bank EFG Ltd. The banker's payment is sent forthwith in the EFG section of the daily remittances.

Before the banker's payment is presented to the EFG Bank, it is announced that all payments by Merchant Bankers ABC Ltd have been suspended, and in due course the banker's payment is returned by the EFG Bank to the XYZ Bank, Anytown Branch, with the answer 'Refer to Drawer'..

What action should the XYZ Bank take and what are its rights?

The problem centres around the nature of a banker's payment, which, for the purpose of stamping legislation it will be observed is described as a 'draft or order drawn by any banker in the United Kingdom upon any other banker in the United Kingdom, not payable to bearer or to order, and used solely for the purpose of settling or clearing any account between such bankers' (Stamp Act, 1891, Bill of Exchange exemption (2)). Also it is to be observed that *for the purpose of the payment of a crossed cheque* pursuant to Section 79 of the Bills of Exchange Act, 1882, it was held in the case of *Meyer & Co. Ltd.* v. *The Sze Hai Tong Banking and Insurance Co. Ltd.* (1913) A.C. 847, it was held in the House of Lords that cheques given in exchange by a banker to a presenting banker were in fact payment. Whether in the event of such banker's payment not being met, the giving of such cheque constitutes final payment leaving the loss with the recipient does not necessarily follow. That is, however, not a point that has to be determined *specifically* in order to answer the above question.

It will be observed that the XYZ Bank has discounted a bill which, at maturity, is presented for payment, paid in so far as the issue of a banker's payment amounts to payment, but that the banker's payment is not met because of the failure of the bank concerned. The thought

185

N

that one could not stop a banker's payment was eliminated many years ago in that where small bankers had issued payments and then failed their clearing agents were generally admitted as having no liability to meet such payment.

As between parties to a bill, payment would not seem to be effected if in fact the cheque issued therefor or the bankers payment issued therefor is dishonoured. At one time it was commonplace for bankers to require a bill of exchange to be attached to a cheque if in fact they were asked to accept a cheque as payment from a commercial firm. Where such cheque was dishonoured there was no suggestion that the bill itself had been paid. It may have been that the attachment of the cheque to the bill amounted only to conditional payment. Nevertheless, the general principle that payment by a cheque or a draft is conditional would normally be expected to apply in all instances. That is to say, that in the same way as where a cheque is given for the payment of an ordinary debt and the cheque is dishonoured the debt still outstands, so it is logical to draw the conclusion that the bill has not been paid, the possible exception being in the case indicated above as between bankers for the purpose of the Bills of Exchange Act.

The question arises as to what action the XYZ Bank should take. As holder of the bill it will give notice and note within the requirements of Section 49 of the Bills of Exchange Act and so long as it acts diligently it is difficult to see how in any way its rights against the parties liable on the bill are going to be adversely affected. This does not mean, however, that such bank could not in the alternative agree to treat the bill as paid and claim in the insolvency of the defaulting bankers if it were thought that this course would be advantageous, having regard to the respective financial position of the parties concerned. Thus, to summarise, the XYZ Bank should treat the bill as dishonoured. By doing so it would not appear to affect its own legal rights to claim also against the defaulting bankers in due course, although this possibility cannot be ruled out.

Probably the best guidance is from the case of *London Banking Corp. Ltd. v. Horsnail, Hayward & Cooper* (1898) 14 T.L.R. 266. The facts were somewhat similar and in giving judgment Mr Justice Bingham recalled that instead of insisting on cash for the bill, a banker's payment had been taken, accepted, but not honoured. There had not, however, in his view been payment 'in fact' because the banker's payment received had not been converted into cash. Therefore it is perhaps reasonable to conclude that by taking a banker's payment, (*i*) there is no question of the acceptor being released, and (*ii*) there is, however, the possibility that third parties may be regarded as being released because the delay in giving notice or noting and protesting as the case may be could have been avoided.

3 : Revoking a credit transfer

North Bank, York, remit on 8 January under a banker's order instruction a credit transfer for £200 to the account of the XYZ Company Limited at South Bank, Oxford. This credit transfer duly reaches Oxford, through their head office, on 10 January.

On 9 January, North Bank, when posting in their ledgers the work of the 8th, realise that their customer has no funds available and to rectify their mistake immediately write to South Bank, Oxford, requesting that this credit be refunded to them. In consequence, both this letter and the credit transfer reach Oxford in the morning mail of 10 January.

North Bank maintain that at this stage the credit is still in course of transfer and consequently they are entitled to demand its return. South Bank however maintain that as this is not an 'advance' standing order payment the funds are now under their control and in this they have a duty towards their customer.

What should North Bank's attitude be?

Most of those answering the question recognized that in practice the problem would be likely to be resolved through a spirit of co-operation. Normally, quite apart from the legal position, the recipient banker, that is the South Bank at Oxford in the question, will be willing to pay back the money. Such an attitude may be prompted by sympathy, or by the thought of the need for future reciprocity. It is probable that, in fact, a telephone call would have been made by most bank managers on the day on which the mistake was discovered, in the case mentioned, on 9 January. The alacrity with which the recipient bank responds may be affected by the existence of an out-of-order debit position which would be remedied by the credit. Otherwise, unless the manager of the recipient branch fears that his customer may know and demur, the prospect of refund is strong. This, however, may not be the proper course and is certainly no answer to the question, which, fundamentally, is a matter of law.

The question is a difficult one from a legal aspect, mainly because the credit transfer system has not been the subject of litigation. Although the law relating to payment in mistake of fact has some relavance to the problem, the first point to clarify is the status of the recipient banker. The view taken depends upon whether the recipient bank is the agent of his customer or the agent of the party directing that the payment be made. This is a subject upon which there is a divergence of opinion. Clearly if the recipient bank receives a cheque or a payment and is the agent of the payor then there is a right of recall. If this is not so, and the recipient bank is the agent of its own customer, the law relating to payment in mistake of fact becomes relevant.

The normal conception of the position of the recipient banker is that he is an agent for his customer. There is no doubt that when a cheque is paid in for collection he is acting as agent. If the payment-in is at a nearby branch the same position obtains. If the payment-in is at another bank, that other bank is an agent of the ultimate recipient bank. This is the traditional basis that bankers have regarded as the background of such daily transactions. There is, however, another view. The clearing bankers have publicised the credit transfer system by advertisement. Such an advertisement may be regarded as an open offer to the public. Many years ago an advertiser offered a cold-cure to the public with financial payment in the event of failure (*Carlill* v. *Carbolic Smoke Ball Co.* (1893) 1 Q.B. 296). It was held that the mere use by a member of the public who had seen the offer created the contract. If this principle applies to the utilisation of the credit transfer system it may be considered that the recipient bank – being one of the group that advertised – was acting on behalf of the person seeking to recall the payment. In that event the question of payment in mistake of fact would not be relevant. Both banks would be holding on behalf of the payor until the account of the recipient is actually credited. The money would then have to be returned to the relevant bank. Whether this position obtains may be dependent on the particular facts. Perhaps the better view is that the recipient bank is the agent of its own customer. If this is not the case then it is to be noticed, in passing, that a number of other problems may arise – such as whether, if a cheque was involved, the collecting banker is protected against conversion and/or has recourse in that event or in the event of the cheque being dishonoured.

If the recipient bank is in fact an agent of the customer the problem is one of payment in mistake of fact (with which our respondents dealt adequately). Perhaps the dominant factor is that the mistake must be as between the payor and the recipient – that is to say, the same mistake must have been made by both. Banking students may remember the

189

case of *Chambers* v. *Miller* (1862 13 C.B.N.S. 123) in which the mistake was on the part of the payor and recovery was not permitted because the mistake – as to whether there was sufficient balance to pay – was not *between* the payor and the recipient. In the present instance, *even presuming that the recipient bank is in law the agent of its own customer and not of the bank from which the money is received,* we still do not know the precise facts. If the payment is being recalled because the money was paid through a one-sided mistake with which the ultimate recipient was not concerned, then recovery is not possible because of the above-mentioned principle. If both parties were under the same mistaken impression, then it is recoverable. There is however an exception. If the immediate recipient is an agent who has paid over to his principal, then recovery cannot be obtained from the agent (*Kerrison* v. *Glyn Mills Co.* (1911, 105 L.T. 721). In the case under consideration this would not appear to be so. Again, the special rules preventing recovery where payment is of a negotiable instrument that has been transferred would not appear to be applicable.

Therefore, to summarise legally, if the credit transfer system is regarded as having operated as an open offer, then recovery by South Bank is possible because both banks are acting for the payor. If, as is probably the case, the recipient bank is the agent of its own customer, then recovery will only be possible legally if the mistake has arisen from circumstances about which both the payor and the ultimate recipient are mistaken. Even then, had South Bank altered its position on the strength of the payment, there may have been no recovery.

4 : Credit transfer on the strength of a cheque

Bloggs Ltd is a mail order company which has adopted the credit transfer system at the behest of its bankers, Lowtown Bank Ltd, Anytown branch. Invoices of Bloggs Ltd have a slip attached which its client can use to pay in money at any branch bank.

John Smith calls at the Anytown branch of the bank and, using the credit slip provided, pays in his cheque in favour of Bloggs Ltd drawn on Hightown Bank Ltd, in another town, for the credit of Bloggs Ltd. The credit is accepted by Lowtown Bank Ltd and Bloggs Ltd receives an advice on the next business day and the company releases goods to Smith.

The cheque is returned unpaid some days later with a bad answer and Bloggs Ltd seeks to recover the amount from Lowtown Bank Ltd, on the grounds that it understood the credit transfer system related to cash transactions only. The company claims that in the case of a bank customer sending a cheque with the credit transfer slip to his own bank, the proceeds would be automatically cleared when credited to the account of Bloggs Ltd. What is the position of Lowtown Bank Ltd?

It is to be emphasised at the outset that the 'credit transfer system' has not been the subject of litigation and that, therefore, views expressed are more than usually open. The 'traders credit method', from which the system differs only slightly and which has been operative for a generation or more, has similarly been considered very little, if at all, by the courts. Again, as will be seen, the position may be affected by the wording used in any particular case in the form given to the customer or, of course, in any exchange of correspondence between the customer (Bloggs Ltd) and the Lowtown Bank.

It is reasonable to approach the problem on the basis of first examining the function of the Lowtown Bank Ltd. If a cheque is paid in by a customer for the credit of his account there is no doubt that the bank is the customer's collecting agent. It is also established that, although the collecting banker may credit a cheque to the customer's account immediately on receipt, if the cheque is returned unpaid the customer may be debited. That is the ordinary law of principal and agent as well as banking practice. It is also known that the customer has no right to draw against the cheque until it is cleared but that, sometimes more than general managers would wish, customers are permitted to do so. In some instances even such practice may grow up and be very near to a course of dealing on which a customer may seek to rely, although this would be very rare because a manager will invariably insist on examining such cheques *if* he would be unwilling to grant the customer an unsecured overdraft for the amount concerned.

Where such a cheque is paid in at another branch then, *prima facie,* the bank is still the agent of the customer. It is the one institution and distinction between branch and branch relates only to the drawing of cheques [one of the decisions in the famous *Savoury Case* (1932 2 K.B. 122) was a refusal to accept the suggestion that the knowledge of one branch where the customer kept his account need not be applied if another branch was used to pay-in a cheque]. Where a different bank is used then there is an agency in law. The facility is made known to the customer and he pays in credits at another bank, because perhaps there is no branch of his own bank in the locality. Here again the relationship is clearly one of agency – between the customer and his bank and between the two banks.

The credit transfer system may be wider because of what may have been offered by the bank to the customer or because of what may be said on the transfer form used by Bloggs Ltd and known to and permitted by the bank. If, as is likely, the Lowtown Bank merely receives the cheque as agent for Bloggs Ltd, then the question arises as to whether the advice to Bloggs Ltd differs by wording or by implication from the ordinary advice of a credit. If a credit is advised and Bloggs are told that it is cash, that is one thing; if they are told that a cheque has been received for their credit, that is another, since they know that cheques may be dishonoured; if they have been told that a credit transfer system credit has been received *and expressly or impliedly* they have been told that only cash (or perhaps only cash or cheques drawn on the branch where the credit is paid in) will be received then they are entitled to presume that they will *not* be redebited with the cheque.

It is possible, but doubtful, that in some cases the Lowtown Bank may not receive as agent for the customer but as the result of an offer made to the public generally. If that is so, it is submitted that the answer will still turn on what the bank offers to accept (cash, etc.) coupled with any variation by what the customer may be told in the advice of credits, generally or specifically, by the bank.

192

5 : A customer awaiting trial

John Smith, a bookmaker's clerk, has a small account at the X Bank in Newcastle, the credit balance having never been more than £100. One day Smith pays in £800 in £1 notes. Before the balance is withdrawn the bank is informed that Smith is being charged with receiving £900 from the proceeds of a smash and grab raid. Meanwhile a cheque for £750 is presented for payment drawn by Smith in favour of a car sales firm from whom he has taken delivery of a car. Should the bank pay the cheque? Would it make any difference if the money had been paid into the account of Jones, Smith's brother-in-law, and the cheque had been drawn by Jones?

This question provides an element of contrast between what appears to be the strict legal position and the practical situation. There is a difference in looking at a question in the abstract and that of a branch manager in, say, a medium-sized country town. The circumstances may be such that the events are common knowledge in the district and a large part of the business community, solicitors, bankers, police and many others presume that there is no doubt that the bank will find some ground for refusing payment – a thought that may be more pre-dominant locally if the car firm, who are the payees of the cheque, are many miles away and have no local connections. First, it is pro-posed to examine the legal position and then to attempt to envisage the practical possible alternatives for the banker who is understandably concerned about local opinion.

The legal position of the banker is clear in that the payment of the cheque cannot involve him in any loss. It has to be remembered that John Smith has not been charged. There is *prima facie* evidence of his guilt and also an indication that the stolen money may have been paid into the bank. When money is paid into a bank a debt (to the extent of the credit balance) is created from the bank to the customer. Although the customer may have no title to the notes that he has stolen and paid into the bank, the bank itself being a *bona fide* transferee for value is unaffected. The value is the creation of the debt. In fact the notes may well have been paid out by the bank to another customer. Two old

193

legal cases are relevant. In *Tassell* v. *Cooper* (1850 14 L.T. (O.S.) 466) a farm bailiff received a cheque for £180 in payment for wheat belonging to his former employer which he had wrongfully sold in his own name. He paid the cheque into his own account. The banker under an indemnity refused to honour the drafts that he drew on his account. It was held that, even although the bailiff had improperly obtained the cheque, he could claim payment from his bankers. This does not mean, of course, that the third party wrongfully deprived cannot bring an action to trace the proceeds to the bank account and recover them. This possibly, however, does not affect the legal liability of the banker to pay his customer's cheques from the credit balance. In fact, if he does not do so he will be liable for damages if the money has not been stolen by Smith. All the more is the bank liable if the account of the account of the brother-in-law is used. It is not as if a cheque had been paid in and may have been converted. It is merely the question as to the extent that the customer Jones had knowledge. If Smith is innocent the point is irrelevant. If Smith turns out to be guilty it does not necessarily mean that Jones is involved. When cash is paid into an account there cannot, of course, be any conversion. Another case illustrates the attitude of the courts to monies paid into a customer's banking account. In *Fontaine-Besson* v. *Parr's Banking Co.* (1895, 12 T.L.R. 121) the bank were sued with the object of obtaining an injunction against them to prevent their honouring cheques drawn by the wife of the plaintiff. He alleged that she had stolen money from him and deposited it in a banking account. The court declined to grant an injunction but indicated that she might have been prevented from drawing cheques, although the bank would not be prevented from paying them. If the bank knows of such an injunction against a customer then – according to the terms of the court order – it may be able to claim that there is a legal objection. However, such instances have to be treated with care.

The practical situation will of course depend on its particular circumstances. If Smith wishes to withdraw cash the bank could pay, technically speaking; if they refused the damages may be small if Smith were found 'not guilty'. However, the failure to pay him cash could have consequences causing damages if the money were wanted for a special purpose. There could be no damage for libel if, as likely, no third party was informed – technically speaking even if an answer were written on the cheque there would be no 'publication'. However, in the present case the cheque is drawn in favour of the car sales firm

194

who would re-possess the car if the cheque were to be dishonoured. There may also be damage for libel if the answer is written. Thus, despite local embarrassment, the banker will be in difficulty if he dishonours the cheque. If the party from whom the cash was stolen seeks a court injunction preventing Smith from withdrawing funds it may well be granted. That depends on the discretion of the Court. If the banker has notice that such an application is being made he will run little or no risk in dishonouring the cheque during the 48 hours likely to be involved. The answer is not beyond doubt but the better view is that if he returned the cheque 'Please re-present – Notice of application for Injunction' he would not be sued successfully if the injunction were not obtained. If he approaches the solicitors for the person from whom the monies were stolen, he runs a risk of breach of secrecy. However, the approach will often be made *to* the banker from the solicitors. It is to be stressed that maximum care has to be exercised in such event and the manager should seek legal guidance.

6 : A safe custody problem

The six members of the staff of the Loamshire Bank at the small town of Fordwych enter for a football pools competition. About 3.30 pm on the following Wednesday they learn that they have won some £7,000 between them and liquid refreshment is obtained from a friendly publican. In the course of the rejoicing the manager and the chief clerk omit to lock either of the doors to the safe. The front door of the branch is, however, locked when the staff depart. That evening a petty thief breaks the glass of a door at the back of the building and is amazed to find the safe open. Stupefied by his good fortune he seizes the first deed box and makes away with it. Although there is an ultimate chance of catching the thief, this aspect is in doubt. The box belongs to Farmer Giles and is labelled 'Contents unknown to the bank'. The farmer's lawyer informs the bank that the box contained the following:

(1) £3,000 in £1 notes that the farmer had put aside 'for a rainy day',

(2) Sixty 'Penny Blacks', ten of which are in mint condition, catalogue value claimed to be £600, which had been given to the farmer by his grandfather.

(3) The deeds of the farm.

(4) Correspondence embarrassing to the farmer between him and a former milkmaid, now a happily married woman (and grandmother) living in the town.

Has the bank any liability? Upon what basis is the amount of damage likely to be assessed if in fact the bank is held to be liable?

The first points are, of course, whether a bank has a liability for safe custody and the degree of care that the banker is under a duty to exercise. For many years past there have been legal discussions as to whether the banker is a gratuitous bailee or a bailee for reward. This was important because on some readings of the law, perhaps the better ones, the gratuitous bailee had to exercise a smaller degree of care than a bailee for reward. In practice the problem on this subject has been considerably minimised by the fact that the normal degree of care taken by a banker of articles deposited for safe custody was such that even if he had been regarded as a bailee for reward his duties would have been fulfilled. This is assuming that a bailee for reward had in fact higher duty of care than a gratuitous bailee. The point about which the discussions arose was whether the keeping of a current account was sufficient commercial benefit to make the banker a bailee for reward. In the case of *Giblim* v. *M'Mullen* (1868) LR 2 PC 317 it was held that the bank were gratuitous bailees where there was no payment for accommodation. These days banks may make charges for such space in which event they would be bailees for reward, but – upon the above basis – it would make no practical difference because normally the care taken is sufficient to meet the responsibility resulting from either category of bailment.

The care that the banks normally take, which is the same care they take of their own cash securities, is sufficient answer and the bank would have no liability. This is thought to be so even for gelignite raids, since there is no absolute liability and there is no suggestion that a bailee for even normal reward has an obligation to take steps to protect the items from such unusual forms of theft.

However, in the present instance the cause, and the fundamental cause, of the loss was the negligence by the bank. Had the safe been locked in the normal way the petty thief would not have been able to steal the farmer's box. The bank is thus responsible for loss that follows. The relationship between the bank and the farmer is one of contract. There the measure of loss is that which either was known to the bank by reason of the bank being aware or specific circumstances or consequences that might reasonably be expected to result from the loss of the box. Therefore the category for which a claim may be made would undoubtedly include (*a*) cash, (*b*) deeds, and (*c*) (quite reasonably) valuable postage stamps. It is very doubtful whether the possibly remote consequences of the loss of personal correspondence would be regarded within the compass of damage normally flowing from the breach of contract with the bank.

In each case, of course, there is again the evidence. The farmer's word would no doubt be taken as to the cash – perhaps by the income tax inspector as well as by the bank! It is true that the farmer was losing deposit interest, but there may be reasons other than ones relating to income tax offences for cash being kept in a box. Again, the existence of the deeds would be equally easily accepted. The loss of the stamps might require some third party evidence as to where they came from, but it is thought that there would be little difficulty in their existence

197

being proved. Whilst the existence of the embarrassing correspondence could no doubt be proved by the evidence of the lady concerned, this would obviously considerably exacerbate the position and at all events, as mentioned above, it is thought that the loss of the correspondence would be too remote to form the basis of an action.

Thus the bank would have to pay :

(*i*) the £3,000, together perhaps with interest from the date of loss if the farmer felt that the history of his possession of the money was sufficiently unblemished for the assertion to be made :

(*ii*) The cost of new deeds would probably be nominal – twenty-five to fifty guineas – perhaps even the title might be registered;

(*iii*) The stamps would easily be valued, although catalogue value, the price to a purchaser, would be unlikely to be awarded.

The strength of this answer is reinforced by the decision of *Port Swettenham Authority* v. *T. W. Wu & Co*. (The Times 21st Feb 1978) in which it was decided that, whether or not the bailees were paid, there was an obligation upon them to show that they were not negligent.

Banker and Customer Relationship and The Accounts of Personal Customers *by L. C. Mather* (Fifth revised edition – 1977). A survey designed to aid the practical banker and student in his daily dealings with personal, as opposed to incorporated, customers.

The Accounts of Limited Company Customers *by L. C. Mather* (Fourth edition – 1978). A practical guide for both current and future bankers on the nature, formation and winding-up of a company, as well as operations on the account and security and support for advances.

The Lending Banker *by L. C. Mather* (Fifth revised edition – 1979). A concise and clear picture for the branch manager of the general principles of bank lending.

Securities Acceptable to the Lending Banker *by L. C. Mather* (Fourth revised edition – 1979). A review of the practical and legal aspects of the securities which are acceptable to the lending banker; the book should be of assistance to those responsible for obtaining and perfecting security to safeguard the position of their bank.

Bankers References *by A. W. Wright* (First edition – 1976). A guide which, in approach, is both practical for branch bankers and theoretical for students, and states the basic principles involved in the difficult and delicate task of giving a reference.

Lending Guides – Parts I and II (Second revised edition – 1980). A card index system of lending proposition formulae devised for the benefit of bank managers, who have to learn the art of lending.

Model Answers
Volume 1 – The Practice of Banking (First edition 1978)
Volume 2 – Monetary Theory and Practice (First edition 1979)
Volume 3 – Law relating to Banking (First edition 1979)
Volume 4 – Finance of Foreign Trade and Foreign Exchange (First edition 1979)
Volume 5 – Accountancy (First edition 1979)
—These five volumes comprise guides, but not official answers, to questions set in the Institute of Bankers Examination Papers (April 1970 – September 1976).

To order, or for further information about any of these titles, please contact:—
Publishing Division.,
Waterlow (London) Limited,
Holywell House,
Worship Street,
London EC2A 2EN.